THE
PLEASURES
OF AGE

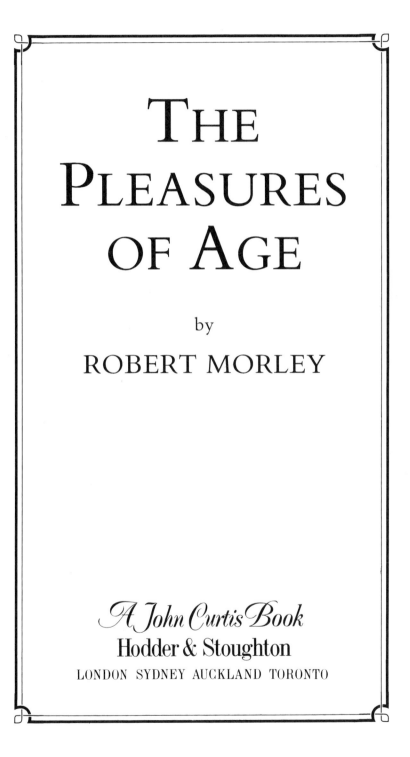

THE
PLEASURES
OF AGE

by

ROBERT MORLEY

A John Curtis Book
Hodder & Stoughton
LONDON SYDNEY AUCKLAND TORONTO

British Library Cataloguing in Publication Data

Morley, Robert, *1908–*
    The pleasures of age.
    I. Title
    828'.91207

    ISBN 0-340-43036-2

First printed 1988.

Published by Hodder & Stoughton,
a division of Hodder and Stoughton Limited,
Mill Road, Dunton Green, Sevenoaks, Kent TN13 2YE
Editorial Office: 47 Bedford Square, London WC1B 3DP.

Photoset by Rowland Phototypesetting Limited,
Bury St Edmunds, Suffolk

Printed in Great Britain by St Edmundsbury Press Limited,
Bury St Edmunds, Suffolk

For my darling wife,
an abiding pleasure

ACKNOWLEDGMENTS

The publishers wish to thank the author and Chatto and Linnit Ltd for supplying the pictures used in this book. They have tried to find the copyright holders wherever possible and are grateful to the following for permission to reproduce particular photographs: David Rudkin (page 17); GTO films (stills from *Too Many Chefs* on pages 49 and 65); Fox Photos (page 71); BBC Hulton Picture Library (pages 75 and 113); the *Daily Telegraph* (photo by Beck, page 95); Mr Michael Noakes PPROI, RP (the reproduction of his portrait on page 109); and the *Sunday Express* (page 125).

CONTENTS

Introduction

Ready to bestow advice

INTRODUCTION

> *"Old age isn't so bad when you consider the alternative."*
> MAURICE CHEVALIER

LEFT ALONE with a pocket calculator I always try to work out the exact number of seconds I have spent on earth. I know the figure would provide me with immense satisfaction but I have never managed to achieve a satisfactory answer, being not naturally adept at motivating the simplest computer. But there is no question – eighty is the watershed. All other birthdays pale beside it. So the day has arrived.

There is one other problem. I have, during the last few years, become increasingly fond of telling people my age. Getting on for eighty, nearly eighty, eighty in a month or so. I have become increasingly deaf to remonstrations (and indeed deaf to many other things). In any case, there is little anyone wants or is able to say in reply, except to express mild disbelief or insincere congratulations. After all, it is not a privilege everyone wants to share. To draw a high card in the lottery of life is not always a blessing. The old grow ill and sometimes stay that way. Those who find life has been too long will dispute the title of this book and dread that it may be thrust into their hands by a well-meaning relative. I apologise. Nor do I deny that there may be aches, fears and pain. I am concerned, but not in this book. Here I strive only to list the pleasures of survival of not necessarily the fittest but the happiest, who every morning, when the sun rises, are pleased to be alive anticipating its shining.

But, I wonder, am I going to go on telling people I am eighty, or soon will be eighty-one, or I am in my middle eighties? Oh, I do hope not. Longevity has been achieved. It is now a cup on the mantelpiece. If I wish, I can take it down, in secret, and give it a rub. I will sit quietly and smile and wait another twenty years for the monarch's telegram, if she manages to send one: no one else can.

This book is dedicated to those who enjoy growing old and are lucky enough to be able to do so.

Eighty years is a long time to enjoy life. Returning from a visit to a phrenologist many years ago, I told my mother that the shape of my head indicated that I had had a difficult birth.

"The difficulty was mine," she replied, with a slight degree of impatience.

If only I had known then what fun life was going to be, I am sure I would have managed my entry without the aid of forceps.

I have met those who think they would have been happier born in other centuries and a few who maintained they had been, but there can be no argument surely that the elderly have never had it so good. Meals on wheels, whether delivered to the door or brought home from the great supermarkets and cautiously reheated on the Aga, provide novelty, sustenance and, even more important, conversation for the elderly consumers.

"Have you tried the salmon mousse, the chicken Kiev, the bread and butter pudding, the beef stew with dumplings, the fishcakes?"

Such questions send us scurrying in all directions at the instigation of friends and neighbours. There are of course some who into age will insist on cooking for themselves. My distinguished mother-in-law, Gladys Cooper, was still making curries and marmalades up to the month she died. She, however, refused to believe that being in her eighties was any different from being in her forties, and while the marmalade was setting would take herself off to the theatre and perform as usual. On a visit to a cinema for a matinée she heard, apparently for the first time, the term 'OAP'. Asked whether she proposed to avail herself of the concession she replied she preferred as usual a seat in the stalls.

Nevertheless, it is the duty of my generation to acquaint ourselves with the privileges now afforded. To travel free on buses, to enjoy the bargain of reduced rail travel, to claim reductions in income tax and increases in pensions, to have subscriptions to clubs and trade unions reduced. It is no longer necessary in my case to have the documentary evidence of my age to hand. I am old. I look old. There is no argument even on tram-cars in Atlantic City.

At my local inn, around Christmas time, two senior citizens can be fed for the price of one. We old ones should always be on the look-out for bizarre privileges not afforded to junior mortals.

But of course it is indoors with the chain cautiously latched to exclude the bogus adventurer that the real pleasures for the old exist as never before. Visiting a friend at this same festive season I remarked on the splendour of the decorations and particularly the small red lanterns that took their place among the holly and paper chains. My host explained that they served the dual purpose of permanent festivity and reassurance. As long as the lamps went on blinking he knew the security arrangements were fully functional.

How different is the age in which we are now fully mature from the previous one in which we read and knitted and chatted up the canary. Now we search for the moment when we can safely take our eyes from the television screen displaying Sir Robin or the hired cassette of our once favourite movie,

Gladys and me reading the phone book

to remove the Cornish pasty from the cardboard and alert the microwave oven.

Mankind took a rocket to the moon and brought back word processors and telephones to be carried from room to room. It seems to me time they were off once more. In a few years, I am sure, robots will provide the perfect companions. They will play games, make the tea, bark like a dog when the house is left unattended and, should intruders gain access, they will record their appearance, note what is being removed and by how many, and will then summon assistance, should they linger.

There is indeed much pleasure in looking forward to such advances as well as looking back, but for the moment I am grateful to many for providing pleasure in my age. To the press who work so hard to catch my attention; to the writers who provide me with detective novels or the account of murders committed in the distant past – murders long forgotten but not by me. What really happened at the Villa Madeira, or Rillington Place or the mean street in Liverpool or the homes of Lizzie Borden and Gaston Dominici?

I am grateful to the racehorse owners and trainers who work so hard to keep me amused, and indeed to the horses themselves; to Steve Davis who keeps me up past my bedtime; to the butcher, the baker and the electronic engineer.

I am aware, of course, that many of my contemporaries find their pleasures elsewhere – on mountain tops or in the depths of the sea; in pursuing the elusive or in appreciating the simple. I am happy to contemplate their endeavours while usually having no desire to participate.

There is, however, not the slightest doubt in my mind that poltergeists attack over seventy. Who else would bother to hide the cheque-book, conceal the one letter that needed answering, deposit one's hearing-aid in the dustbin or push one's spectacles under the chair? But one learns to live happily with the phenomenon, as well as with dust. One learns not to resent falling asleep in front of the television, not to worry unduly where one last saw one's spectacles. They will turn up. Even my hearing-aid, swept up with the dead rose petals, chirped triumphantly in the dustbin until reclaimed. The pleasures of reclamation are not diminished.

When I started this book I was told that Cicero had already dealt with the subject *circa* 44 BC. I found that besides a shared tendency to drop names, he was continually offering advice on how to keep slaves under control and extolling his friends whose mental faculties were still in working order. It is time, I told myself, that a fresh mind should be brought to bear on the subject. I imagine over the last two thousand years, give or take a decade, Cicero has sold more copies than I shall, but I am grateful to my own publisher for having refused to be daunted. Above all I am grateful to my daughter-in-law, Margaret Morley, who, if truth be told, encouraged and collected my own views on these matters and arranged them in some sort of order. The pleasure of having a daughter-in-law such as her outweighs, in my opinion, any advantage Cicero may have had by being first on the campus.

I
Awaking on Retiring

I like to arrive in vintage style

I
AWAKING ON
RETIRING . . .

> *"I grow old ever learning many things."*
> SOLON

ONE OF the great pleasures of the old is the belief that now is the time to start something new. When I was over seventy I suggested to my children that they should abandon their various careers and join me in concentrating on the problem of marketing toothpaste in an aerosol can. Alas, they never took my advice and now others have perfected the method and reap the reward. But it was surely I who first thought of the plan. Other inspirations are too difficult to market – for instance the abolition of one-way streets; the outlawing of cellophane and any other wrapping; the demand that whenever a film or television director avails himself of a flashback on our screens a caption to that effect should be superimposed. I find it extremely irritating to observe my heroine lying in bed suffering from some terminal illness and the next moment discover her cavorting amidst the wild parsley. If the situation is not explained to me by my wife I grow increasingly frustrated.

Although completely happy about these bees in my own bonnet I am not always as tolerant about the buzzing from other hives.

"You want to watch out when Dorothy starts to talk about her fur farm," I was once advised by a fellow member of the cast of a play in which I was acting.

"What will happen?" I asked.

"Just get out of the way fast before she pulls a knife and starts to skin you."

Later in the run the lady complained of fatigue. "Been seeing my solicitor about my fur farm." As I made my entrance I anticipated the sting between the shoulder blades. Until the play closed I was apprehensive that she might lose control. I was surprised but reassured when she retired from the stage soon afterwards and devoted herself to her real calling – the breeding of minks, just north of Toronto.

The elderly discover their true vocation on retiring. Closer to home, in my own county of Berkshire, there resides an ex-colonel who produces from his very own bushes thousands of bottles of gooseberry wine each year. Field Marshal Allenby, after retiring from the exertions of expeditions in Bechuanaland, Zululand, and leading the Egyptian Expeditionary Forces in Gaza, established an aviary in the small garden of his London home where he could contemplate humming-birds when he wasn't off doing some serious fishing. I'm not quite sure what the noted film critic C. A. Lejeune did with herself after her retirement, but she told me that she breathed a sigh of relief and never again went into a cinema. Sir James Crichton Brown, who at the age of thirty-five was appointed to the curiously named post of Lord Chancellor's Visitor in Lunacy – but then it was 1875 – finally retired from the exalted position at the age of eighty and became a best-selling author with a string of books full of humorous reminiscences about his charges. Until he was seventy-eight Algernon Blackwood devoted himself to writing scores of books but then he took to telling ghost stories on television and became a recognisable apparition on his own account. Air Chief Marshal Hugh Dowding took the opposite trail. He led fighter command during the Battle of Britain but retired shortly after to bury himself in the study of theosophy and spiritualism.

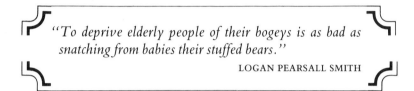

"To deprive elderly people of their bogeys is as bad as snatching from babies their stuffed bears."

LOGAN PEARSALL SMITH

There are those, of course, in public life especially, who upon retirement are reluctant to do without the pressures of their active years and so throw themselves wholeheartedly into community involvement. Next to those who have won the pools and assure us that it will make no difference to their lifestyle is the booby who tells us that he is much busier than he ever was, now that he has retired. It means he is going to be a perfect menace for years on the parish council opposing the installation of traffic signals in the high street, reclaiming rights of way, refusing to fill up the chalk pits and generally making a nuisance of himself over other people's requests for building permission. The Englishman's attitude to property is summed up in the phrase 'dog in the manger'. I myself have a recurring nightmare that a caravan site has sprouted at the bottom of the wood beyond our garden and fierce gypsies are forever crossing and recrossing the land, carrying iron bedsteads. Sometimes they picnic in the rosebed. It is not strictly speaking a pleasure until one wakes to find the green woodpecker busily weeding the grass. I would not wish, I suppose, to discourage the elderly from the pleasure of interfering, or at least trying to do so, in affairs which manifestly are none of their business.

In the correspondence column of my local paper, among the

constant protests about the siting of a new urinal or the demolition of the local cinema or the lack of a launderette in the town centre, there are frequent references to the desirability of cutting red tape. If it wasn't for the assured presence of the latter, we should be in a sorry state indeed. Any attempt to cut through red tape brings the realisation that the stuff simply doesn't cut. Lawyers tie up their briefs with it and local government ties up everything else. We had a cinema in my local town. Suddenly (or so we thought) it was closed and the elderly ladies who owned this non-profit-making venture were offered untold wealth to sell it to the local supermarket. "*En garde,*" we murmured, and marched. We didn't traverse the ground, however. We bought tickets to innumerable functions; we stood, umbrellas at the ready, to protest outside this palace of entertainment which had seldom before seen a queue, unless a new Bond film was on exhibition. This we told ourselves was a matter of urgency. Now, three years later, for all I know the elderly Devonians still await their fortune, the organ has been removed to a place of safety, and with not a bulldozer in sight the whole adventure is what is known still as 'in the planning stage'. Meanwhile a use has been found for the buses once they have fetched the children from school. They are refuelled and set off once more on a journey of a dozen miles to a new cinema complex which boasts six separate screens and is rapidly becoming our local Glyndebourne.

We are not, in these parts, geared for sudden change and we are back to chores of baking cakes and selling them to each other to relieve famine in Ethiopia or sponsoring our grandchildren to swim untold distances in the local bath in aid of the lifeboat-building programme, though situated as we are a goodly distance from Bournemouth. Every two years or so we steel ourselves for our local Festival. We stretch a banner across the village street and wait hopefully for visitors to descend upon us to view the parade of floats, which are led in procession around the housing estate, headed – and this is where I come in – by the oldest inhabitant who is still just active enough to climb into the vintage car and declare the fête open. After a lifetime spent showing off I enjoy doffing my top hat to anyone placing a contribution in the collecting buckets. I only hope I can still make it when it comes around again. I am not quite as busy as I used to be, though still fighting a scheme to keep yellow lines off the high street. 'Boobyism' must be listed among the pleasures of age.

> *"Old age takes from the intellectual man no qualities save those which are useless to wisdom."*
>
> JOSEPH JOUBERT: *Pensées*

The world is, of course, full of those who for one reason or another cannot face the idea of retirement. Some have no desire to sail the Atlantic, write a book, catch a salmon or plant a vineyard. The idea of organising the village fête or shaking a collecting box appals them. No, what they want to do is what they have always done. This is their pleasure. The actor who times his demise with the fall of the curtain; the poet who spends his life searching for the appropriate word – age does not dim their preoccupation. Katherine Anne Porter was seventy-two when she finally published her acclaimed novel, *Ship of Fools*. It was rumoured she had been working on it for twelve years. Colette was over seventy-two when she wrote her most famous work, *Gigi*. Palmerston was over seventy when he became Prime Minister, although as politicians go that record hardly compares with that of Sir Francis Knollys, who was elected Member of Parliament for Reading in 1640: he was ninety. After a lifetime of campaigning, the American reformer and teacher Susan B. Anthony became president of the National American Suffrage Association when she was seventy-two, a post she held until she was eighty. William Keble Martin, a vicar, spent all his free time studying flowers. Although until he was in his seventies the church left him little leisure for other things, his real passion was the garden. He was eighty-eight when he saw the fulfilment of a lifetime's work with the publication of *The Concise British Flora in Colour*, a great bestseller in its day. Redcliffe Salaman devoted his life to studying potatoes and reached his seventy-fifth birthday before he was ready to publish his findings – *The History and Social Influence of the Potato*. The music critic on the *Observer* for many years, Arthur Henry Fox, was eighty when he dipped into his store of knowledge to begin translating all the songs of Brahms, Hugo Wolf and Richard Strauss. He had almost finished those of Liszt as well when he died nine years later. But for sheer volume of work it is hard to beat Alexander Murison the jurist and author who, after what anyone would call a lifetime as a teacher and at the bar, turned to translating when he was eighty-four and managed the whole of Horace and Pindar into verse, Virgil's *Bucolics* and *Georgics* and the first twelve books of the *Iliad* into English hexameters. William Cullen Bryant also translated the *Iliad* but he was a mere stripling of seventy-six at the time. Sir Bruce Ingram, editor of the *Illustrated London News*, was well into his eighties but still crawling around the floor of his office laying out photographs for the next issue. Although always a respected actor, A. E. Matthews was seventy-eight when he finally achieved stardom as the Earl of Lister in *The Chiltern Hundreds*. He was eighty when he filmed the role. The mathematician Henry Baker published his last paper on geometry when he was eighty-six. James Braid, the golfer, celebrated his eightieth birthday on the Walton Heath course. It was a wet and stormy day and he holed the course in 81.

My own father was a great believer in carrying on, although not for him the history of the potato nor a translation of a Greek epic. For my father it was gambling – a vocation he pursued happily until his death. (The lady who only recently won a million on the pools had the grace to admit that such a sum would substantially alter her lifestyle and that her husband was already contemplating the purchase of a new fishing rod. One thing, however, would remain constant – the weekly task of filling in the coupon.) My father instilled in me two beliefs. First, that there was no family entail ever proposed through which a competent lawyer could not drive a coach and horses and, secondly, that to accumulate one must speculate. Though not himself either a Catholic or a churchgoer, he also had the belief in *Le Bon Dieu*. He would explain his total abstinence from church attendance by the claim that while others were no doubt praying for him, he could utilise the hours more profitably on his family's behalf by mugging up the racing form. With the innocence of the compulsive gambler he also genuinely believed that he would one day triumph at bridge, poker, roulette, on the race track or at one of the other innumerable games of chance which exercised his dreams, and indeed all his waking hours. He was confident that answering the doorbell he would not on this occasion be confronted once again by a bailiff, but rather by the man from Littlewoods or the secretary of the Irish Sweepstake or whoever it is that calls to apprise the winner on these occasions. So great was his optimism, so euphoric his expectations that he still purported to believe, on his deathbed, that his investment in Argentine Railway Bonds would one day be worth a fortune to his heir. "Don't waste it, Bobby," he begged.

His devotion to gambling was only exceeded by his respect for members of the Jockey Club – if he was able to borrow from them. His code of honour told him that Dukes seldom asked for their money back. Bookmakers on the other hand demanded and often received payment; to an extent, but never

Father was always so well turned out

on his scale, I have continued to support the latter. Choose any four horses, couple them in eleven unlikely combinations and you can turn the pages of a morning paper, avoiding the disasters befalling others, and find in the sporting columns that you have won a fortune. I have done it once in sixty years but I am still, to quote father once more, in the ring. The old must never isolate themselves from the Goddess of Chance. For the price of a Premium Bond you have as much chance of the jackpot as the winner. A small entry in the pools, a share in a ticket for the Spanish lottery, a modest stake in your local church lucky-draw and you could gain a fortune – or a small teddy-bear. There are few pleasures more potent than antici-pation and wondering what you would do with the spoils. The teddy-bear one supposes would have to go to the local hospi-tal, but to be as rich as Croesus and not having to pay capital gains tax. Magic!

Gambling, however, is not the only way for the aged to experience the pleasure of expectation. Once, having stalled her vehicle in Goudhurst (I think it was Goudhurst), my sister, as she waited for the motor to unflood, said that she had never cared much for that village.

"The trouble," she opined, "is the lack of PLUs."

I had never heard the expression and queried it.

"People like us, dear," she elaborated.

My dear late sister was, I used to think, wrong about most things but we shared a common delight in watching the television programme the *Antiques Roadshow*, and we were indeed hastening through the dusk to be home in time to watch it, which may have caused her impatience with the starting mechanism on that occasion. The old, who tend to believe that PLUs are an endangered species along with man-eating tigers, will surely take heart whenever the professional valuers in their role of conservationists appear in the pro-gramme. It is not they of course who are the real attraction but the PLUs themselves who emerge from their hiding-places to approach the tethered golden calf. Most suspect, indeed know, that the Mongolian tinder-box they bear so proudly shares its sentimental value with intrinsic worth. No, of course they are not particularly interested in the value placed upon it by the expert. They hadn't, naturally, thought of selling it. The memory of maiden aunt Tilda persists. But perhaps for the sake of insurance it might be rather nice to know – approximately of course. The valuer plays them like a fish. Austrian replicas were almost common in the midst of the eighteenth century. There was a factory in Holstein Uber Loff which turned them out generously. But stay! This one is from the Lodz works of Arbeit Munchel and is a considerable rarity. Indeed the expert has only once before had such an example in his hands. Here the speaker lets out a little of the line. Did they realise the specimen was missing a small section of the glaze and there was a slight discoloration of the patina? Have you any idea of the value? Here the line is taut once more. It might even snap.

"We thought about five hundred pounds."

A good deal more they are assured – "Nearer three thousand."

"Fancy, as much as that."

One wonders if they will resist the temptation. Probably, since People Like Us need at least one nest-egg in the house for reassurance as we get older. For years after I had bought, in Goa of all places, an ivory carving of the boy Jesus, I was convinced it was the work of the late Michelangelo. It came, I decided, from an altar in Tuscany and was the missing detail of a reredos acquired by Duveen from a Tuscan church and then mysteriously lost or more probably pilfered by an Indian butler he once employed at I Tatti or wherever the old dealer holed up. The provenance was authenticated by myself. I told the tale to whoever chanced to pick it up from the mantelpiece where it customarily reclined, someone having detached a foot. For once not wanting too much publicity from television exposure, I avoided the *Antiques Roadshow* and carried my treasure to Sotheby's where I handed it over to a lady who was trying unsuccessfully to wrestle a Stradivarius from the determined grasp of the surviving descendant of the original maker. In the antique market all is fantasy. I waited while the discovery was carried aloft and imagined the scene when the head of the Department of Renaissance Art was alerting his colleagues and presumably the Director of Press Relations as well as the Getty Museum. Sotheby's on this occasion slipped up. I had, so they opined, a very nice little carving from Goa and they would be happy to make me a little case in which our Saviour could stand upright. I accepted the offer. For the sixty-seven pounds they charged, my relic sometimes attracts the attention of fellow connoisseurs.

"The provenance is disputed," I tell them. "One day I must take it along to Christie's."

The pleasures of age must always include the occasional heirloom in the attic, or in my case displayed on a convenient shelf above the curtain. Only yesterday my wife found an item in the newspaper about coronation mugs fetching literally thousands of pounds. I have several and one particularly interesting mug commemorating the opening of the Tay Bridge. Now that surely must be worth a fortune. Then, too, there is that small silver compass recording the distance from Valencia to other cities and fitted with what I take as a sundial. I shall certainly hang on to it for a few more years. Prices are sure to improve and meanwhile I shall occasionally carry it into the garden to try to estimate the correct time in Vienna.

There are those of course whose preoccupation is not so much acquiring money in age as disposing of it. Hugh Graham, for example, the newspaper tycoon who started the *Montreal Star* when he was twenty-one, was still running his empire well into his eighties. Then he gave it up for the pleasure of running soup-kitchens every winter in Montreal. Or James Buchanan who, having started his company on borrowed money, built up a fortune and found pleasure in his old age in disposing of it in two ways. One was on the race-course and in the training stables. At the age of seventy-three he watched his horse, Captain Cuttle, win the Derby. Four years later he was lucky again and Coronach won the famous race. At seventy-eight he was elected to the Jockey Club. Other money he simply gave away – to universities, hospitals, and he actually gave a substantial sum to the King for the restoration of the nave of St George's Chapel, Windsor. There must be great pleasure to be derived from financing the monarch. But as much, I wonder, as from watching your own horse win a race, which is just what James Buchanan did at Worcester two days before his death at the age of eighty-six? And this was a man who was judged to be in delicate health all his life.

On the whole my advice is not to leave your affairs in order. Your heirs and any friends left will have less time for grief if there are many problems to occupy them.

"What I wonder would father have liked us to do with those?" they will ask themselves, contemplating a small library of pornography. Burn? Read? Sell?

To avoid death duties by distributing your fortune is not really very sensible either. The man who made a fortune hiring out television sets or planning housing estates and gives a few million to build a hospital invites suspicion: he has a guilty conscience that all his life he has overcharged people or diddled the tax collector. Notwithstanding, the accumulation of wealth is for many a fascinating hobby. At the outset they may have been motivated by the purest of ambitions – to provide the wife with a mink coat, to own a swimming pool – but later as the jacuzzis proliferate and the gold trickle gathers momentum they find themselves being swept along into foreign bank accounts and tax-free havens. The Revenue only occasionally overtakes the one who got away with a flying start. The result is a famous collection of pictures left to the nation to infuriate the heirs. The avoidance of the inheritance tax by the very rich, the lonely sojourn in the Isle of Man merely reinforces the belief that the leopard seldom changes its spots. The old may genuinely believe it is their duty not to leave their money to the government, who will fritter it away, but they must guard against such intentions becoming obsessive. Of course it may be that such observations flatter those who have borrowed this volume from their local library.

"There are two things to aim at in life: first to get what you want; and, after that, to enjoy it. Only the wisest of mankind achieve the second."

LOGAN PEARSALL SMITH

One of those pleasures which are heightened as we get older is the contemplation of our possessions. By which I do not mean vast acres of Cumbrian peat or the magic number of a Swiss bank account, welcome as these adjuncts to gracious living may be. No, I mean the sort of treasures I possess. Mother's silver sweet-box or Grandmother's sugar-castors. I don't know who thought of joining two wine-coasters with silver vine leaves and combining it with a sprinkler which scatters sugar around the table-cloth. In Grandmother's day there were staff to clear up after her. Everyone needs treasures when the years advance. One's friends are beginning to look terrible but Mother's chocolate box keeps its youth.

'Father' planted the oak trees: one either side of the road just outside our gate. Not my father of course. He was not in any sense a conservationist. It was an old gentleman hermit who lived next to us when we moved in fifty years ago.

"You will live, my boy, to see them shake hands – and now you can stop holding them upright," he said. I did and they have.

I used to think it might be nice to have an indoor swimming pool. Ideally it would be outdoor as well. One would be able to swim straight from the drawing room under a window (closed of course in cold weather) out on to the terrace. Perhaps with a piano on a platform overhead. I had a friend who built himself something on those lines but, alas, after a few months he had transformed himself into a swimming-pool attendant who greeted his guests in rough towelling and was perpetually concerned with condensation. He was always buying expensive ferns and enormous pot plants and became obsessed with the harm done to them by splashing. Nature does not take kindly to medicated water.

Another possession which has caught my fancy from time to time is a lift attached to a stair-rail. I am struck by the almost unnatural happiness of the lady in the advertisement clutching a handbag as she is borne aloft. It is true I no longer enjoy climbing stairs and as yet do not carry a handbag but I have found to my cost that I am also not very nippy when alighting from a chair-lift. Another pleasure in store, and likely to remain there unless prices decrease, is an automatic cover for my own swimming pool: a touch of a remote-control switch and a sort of venetian blind raises itself from the deep end and floats blissfully on the surface. But might it crush an unwary and late bather to death? Better resign myself to lugging the tarpaulin and hoping for the best as regards the inevitable splits. Each year, when I have managed to get the temperature up sufficiently for my first bathe, I reassure myself with my annual underwater length. It is true it is not a particularly large pool but I am aware of triumph.

2
Travelling Hopefully

Not *queuing in Red Square*

2
TRAVELLING
HOPEFULLY . . .

"Grow old along with me!
The best is yet to be,
The last of life, for which the first was made."
ROBERT BROWNING

T HE GREY-HAIRED set have, I notice, acquired an acronym of their own. More and more often articles appear in newspapers and magazines about 'WOOPIES' – Well-Off-Older-People. In America more than 25,000 people are one hundred years or older, and in another decade the number is expected to pass the hundred-thousand mark. In Great Britain fifteen per cent of the population is over sixty-five and those of general retirement age hold forty per cent of the individual wealth of the country. There is, I am assured, a major demographic shift towards the elderly. And what are most of the WOOPIES doing now that the children are off their hands, the mortgage and life insurance paid and responsibilities in general decreasing? A good deal of their new-found time is spent travelling – not so much hand-in-hand into the sunset but more likely with swimsuits and golf clubs into the rising sun in Spain or, guidebook at the ready, trekking in the Himalayas. Although, I suppose, like most of the things I never actually intended to do in the first place, the acquisition of a castle in

Spain where the final sunset could, as it were, be prolonged was never seriously contemplated. For one thing I don't get on particularly well with foreigners. The Greeks, for example. Nevertheless a personage on Corfu once enquired if I was thinking of buying a house in his domain. We were watching a lamentable display of swollen ankles while the local crones hopped up and down in the village square.

"This is the only place in Corfu where you can find this particular routine," Lawrence Durrell informed me.

"I still don't think I would be happy here," I told him.

"Suit yourself," he replied, "but the Taylors are coming. Prices sure to rise."

I am not one for local customs. The sight of a morris dancer has me heading in another direction.

For a long time I had a recurring dream of a house I had, perhaps, once glimpsed. It was in a valley across a road and then across a river. Trying to recapture its peculiar fascination I realise my Shangri La was probably in Tibet, a country I have studiously avoided visiting in this life. But was I once the owner of the property in another? How happily I embarked on those enormous treks. I would walk on through the scenery never glimpsed by others, totally free of anxiety because I realised the return journey would be achieved in the instant of waking.

Nowadays my dreams stay closer to home. Tea with the Queen at Windsor: how well I get on with the Royal Family. But sometimes I am situated in some enormous resort hotel, unable to remember on which floor I will find my bedroom. I am unable to stop the elevator as it climbs remorselessly to the top of the tower block. I have checked out and have only twenty minutes to pack and make for the airport where my plane is waiting – or should be, except that the flight has closed.

Oscar Wilde called the sun the enemy of art. For the old it is their staunchest ally, even when it is not shining overhead. Bournemouth had five hours of sunshine, the weather man reports. He doesn't tell us when. It could have been before we normally are awake. We had our eyes open all day, or very nearly, and never saw the thing at all. We search the paper to find out how they got on in Nice. How would we get on in Nice? Or the Costa Brava? Marrakesh? Should we at this comparatively late hour enlist the sun as our constant ally? We don't want to overdo it. The desert may have charms for Mr Thesiger but not for us. (Besides, he never seems to have basked – just kept pushing his way through the reeds.) But to sit month after month on a verandah staring out to sea under the cloudless sky – surely that would suit. So why have I never accepted an invitation to fly to Barcelona and inspect a brand new condominium nearby, or buy, sight unseen, the lower dungeon of a castle in Fez? I suppose I am not as adventurous as I used to be.

Mother used to winter in Mentone. (We English insisted on pronouncing the final vowel.) Sometimes I would go with her by steamer to Genoa and then, I seem to remember, on by train. There was no one much to talk to, but then Mother seldom spoke to strangers. There was the English Library, the English Tea Rooms, the English Tennis Club, and when one left the ship one carried a complimentary and beautifully carved soap-box. I still have mine.

As soon as Mother untied the apron strings I was off. Once to Majorca, where I fell deeply in love. The object of my passion was accompanied by her elderly and fabulously wealthy husband. He, in his turn, had a passion for boating. At sea, while he slept, we frolicked. Overwhelmed by a feeling of guilt (after all he was paying for the hire of the craft) I planned elopement. I wasn't a very practical sixteen-year-old and only had twenty pounds left after paying my bill. As I waited for her beside the jetty and bargained with the boatman on the first stage of our flight to paradise there was the thought that she would probably bring some of her fairly extensive jewellery collection. I sought reassurance: I opened the note she had left for me at the caisse. Wiser counsel had prevailed, at least where she was concerned. I broke off negotiations with the boatman and ran for the bus. At least I never had to explain to Mother.

Years later we met unexpectedly at the Berkeley Grill. She still had the jewellery but not her husband, as he had died. At least it was she who recognised me. For an hour we spoke, or at any rate she did, on the difficulty of keeping her servants. I comforted myself with the thought that she would not have kept me for long. I put the whole incident down to sunstroke and am careful now to shelter under a tree or a parasol tethered to the table. In the water I wear a hat. Still, I can understand other people opting to float out their lives in Hawaii and then leave instructions that their ashes should be scattered into the Pacific, unheedful of the trouble they cause. It is extremely difficult for friends or relatives to carry out their commands. The wind always seems to get up at the wrong moment.

Am I now too late for pilgrimage? Do I really want to seek Surfer's Paradise again? Was Mr Norman Douglas really happy in Capri? More important, would I be? Condominiums have a habit of leap-frogging to the water's edge. What was once a beach is now, alas, another's bathroom. Venetian blinds are called for. It is curious how often one has to depend on them.

Has one seen enough? Ought one to die without walking on the Great Wall of China? Perhaps in your case the answer is less complicated. Perhaps you have spent a lifetime in the Kalahari, made a solo voyage around the world, taken a dog-sleigh to one or possibly both poles. For me there is a good deal left to do by way of exploration.

It is true I once went to Beijing, but I didn't get to the Wall. I left it to my deputy, a splendid lady of over ninety, who had

One of Mother's prettiest dresses

a thing about ancient monuments. I contented myself with the Winter Palace and the Gates of a Thousand Delights, or whatever. I awaited my emissary's return, the gin and tonic already mixed and the ice tinkling in the glass. She accepted it gratefully.

"The Chinese are lucky to have the Wall," she told me. "It is not anything you could build these days. They thought it would deter Genghis Khan but of course it didn't. Still it must have earned its keep by now with the tourist trade. Tell me about the Palace. Is it true they have a concrete barge floating on the lake?"

I had to tell her the barge was built from the bottom up: even the Chinese aren't that clever. But we both enjoyed the Terracotta Warriors and the complimentary raisins supplied by the airline.

There is a lot to be said for a few weeks in Russia and taking the Siberian Express, which lands you at Nakoda, an easy boat-ride to Tokyo. Waiting for the inevitable suspicion of bureaucracy, I was approached by a fellow-traveller who had been trading illegally in furs and had a packet of hot roubles, which he suggested I changed for him into dollars. Shaking with alarm I saw us both in some remote Siberian prison, until the Intourist guide encouraged me to oblige.

For the elderly there is particular satisfaction in perusing the travel brochures offered to others just before they have caught their breath after Christmas and the January sales. They tick off the destinations they themselves have visited. Not Siberia again, or the Algarve, the Costas, Miami, Venice – not even a week in Dubrovnik or a fortnight in the Seychelles.

There was once a trip to Kenya to watch elephant. "I am rather closer to this herd than I would wish and would prefer you to ignore them" – I can still hear the chilling admonition of the white hunter and recall the same evening when a mammoth took a fancy to my bungalow porch. I asked what would happen if I attempted an early night? If I patted his flank in a goodnight salute? "He would kill you," I was told. It was as simple as that.

Gone are the days when my fellow senior citizens are content with a week in Great Yarmouth. More is expected of them and how nobly they rise to expectations. Aztec ruins, pre-Columbian pottery, Russian icons. There comes a sudden unnatural desire to be instructed in Armenian basket weaving, a longing for a week sighting whales or learning to knit. Watching on television is preferable. I can switch off when tired and refuse to follow another step across the glacier or to wait impatiently for the birth of a lesser newt.

> *"Perhaps being old is having lighted rooms*
> *Inside your head, and people in them, acting.*
> *People you know, yet can't quite name."*
>
> PHILIP LARKIN

I never care to be too close to nature. The undeveloped beach is not for me. I care nothing for the scramble over the barbed wire, the virgin shingle. The absence of other bathers afrights. Currents? Sea snakes? Sharks? When shown the Channel for the first time I was quoted as having remarked: "What a great big bath for Bobbie Morley." I do not recall making the observation. I do, however, remember frantic digging on the beach at Folkestone when I was determined to emigrate to Australia and was resolved to arrive there before tea was called.

I would like to choose Folkestone for a holiday again one day, if only for the meringues, but can one be quite sure they are still available? I remember the shop perfectly but so much changes as one gets older that even Bouverie Road West might have changed direction. An uncle died in Folkestone at the

Metropole Hotel leaving me ten thousand pounds and Mrs Gee once gave me invitations to deliver for a bridge party but my fear of strange dogs impelled me to throw them into the sea. There were lifts that carried one down the cliffs and a terrifying whoosh of water before we were on our way. A famous old actor called Squire Bancroft lived at Sandgate and a lady called Mrs Boddom-Whettam used to take tea. There was never a lack of amusement: the sugar-loaf mountain to climb, the central station was a sort of Disneyland with its automatic machines, and the ski-slope down which we raced in terror lest we would be unable to arrest our headlong flight and be hurled under a bus at the bottom. There was the skating rink and the Leas Cliff Pavilion where afternoon tea was served during the performance, and a score of teapots raised in unison and suspended over the éclairs until the villain was unmasked. Arthur Brough ran the company and Canon Elliot the church. I remember him in his pulpit surrounded by lilies and dressed to match.

"I know God will forgive me," he once began, "if I say something quite personal."

And I was sure He had and was indeed listening. Everyone listened to the Canon – God and the King and Queen no less. How were we to know that one day he would lose his reason and his faith and concentrate his energy on reading murder mysteries and trying to escape from Virginia Water?

How wonderful it would be to go back one day and encounter an ancient mariner propped against his upturned boat and be remembered as the little chap who once was led screaming from the shore when his proposed trip to Australia was aborted.

When one does largely nothing there is need every so often to take a holiday. There seems a reluctance these days for others to pay my fare to Zanzibar. I have, of course, been luckier than some. Occasional journalism and film acting has taken me to a

I was an eager child ready to please

good many places with a complimentary return ticket in my pocket, and even now there is still the jaunt to Hawaii for a television part or to New York for the same reason. It is a pleasure of age to be greeted on the spot with a comfortable chair placed in the shade for the long periods of waiting. But I have never got over the pleasurable shock when I fulfilled my first professional theatrical engagement on finding that someone else was footing the bill to transport me to Weymouth. I spoke only one line but it was obviously up to me to make it count. Indeed I still have the ticket. After Weymouth I ventured farther afield. Ayers Rock was disappointing. The Straits of Magellan extraordinarily exciting with memories of the skill of the pilot manoeuvring the liner within inches of the reefs. The glimpses of polar bears and seals, distracted by the sight of one of my fellow-passengers appearing on the bridge wearing a white mink coat, and yet it was I who as the principal lecturer was supposed to be the star turn.

Those of a certain age often find that someone is willing to pay their passage in exchange for the remembered anecdotes of a lifetime or just to share the acquired knowledge of their years. A noted lawyer, Sir Cecil Carr was eighty-one when he managed to captain a team of the Senior Golfer's Society, putting and driving their way across America. This he combined with learned addresses to the American Philosophical Society and a couple of law schools.

I cannot pretend to have led an adventurous life but travel has brought its share of disasters. In that I am not alone. This can be a particular hazard for the elderly but not usually in such an extreme way as befell William Eames, an authority on water conservation, who all his life was a great traveller. He was, however, seventy-three when on a trip homeward bound from Rangoon he found himself grounded in Algiers. This being in the midst of the Second World War, arrangements were complicated and he only made it home by signing on as a pantryman assistant to a Chinese cook on a small ship.

Moreover, the job had only become available because for-
tuitously the Turkish crew had mutinied. I myself was in my
seventies when I nearly died one night up the Amazon – not, I
hasten to add, from a snake-bite in the rain-forests, but from a
Mickey Finn administered by the proprietor of a local hostelry
after I had complained about our accommodation. I could
have died of thirst in the sand-dunes of the Outback, if I hadn't
been rescued in plenty of time by a bus driver.

"It is extraordinary," he remarked, "how few of you think
of drinking the water in the car radiator."

Perhaps the elderly shouldn't retrace their steps on holidays. I
wasn't exactly on holiday when, losing my way in Wiltshire, I
found myself in the village of Semley and unaccountably
remembered the name of the house where I was born. I traced
the premises without much trouble, rang the doorbell and
introduced myself to no less a celebrity than Julian Bream. I
explained that I first drew breath in the best bedroom and he
courteously invited me inside to make a tour of the house. I
had always imagined we were not exactly in clover as a family
in that vintage year of my birth but was pleasantly surprised. It
was by no means an insubstantial smallholding, although Mr
Bream had splashed out a bit converting the barn or possibly
erstwhile chicken-house, into a music atelier where he also
turned his hand, or more probably a lathe, to the construction
of mandolines and lutes. I caught him the other evening on my
television screen still playing away happily at home, accompanying a celebrated actress reading the occasional sonnet,
although there was no mention, alas, of my birth somewhat
earlier on the same premises. It must be pleasurable indeed
when one's birthplace is decorated by one of those small blue
plaques while one is still alive. Few householders would object
if an enterprising yuppie made the necessary arrangements for
those who had escaped fame, or still hoped to achieve it, and
had the necessary cash? Why wait for a tombstone?

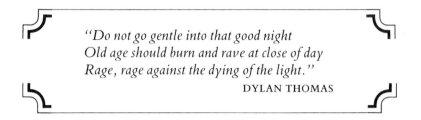

Even though the average age of the population increases annually (by the year 2011 there will be four million people over the age of seventy-five), the elderly should never lose sight of the fact that we are an endangered species. To enjoy life one must always be conscious of predators. The old graze happily, sometimes alone, sometimes in herds. But the wardens lurk. They are for the most part benevolent committee members. Armed with the medicinal dart they occasionally favour anaesthesia and removal to a place of safety. Blanket or netting, ambulance or helicopter, we open our eyes in a nursing home, or perhaps a game reserve, embarking albeit unwillingly on what may prove the last holiday. Resistance may well prove futile but we can fight successfully against the involuntary outing. We do not have to submit to the caring charabanc, the sunset coach bound for Woburn Sands or afternoon tea with an unwary host.

I write from experience having once been prevailed upon to play host to a party of 'over-sixties' (I was at the time seventy-eight) who had hardly crossed the threshhold when they were marshalled into such routine occupations as pulling crackers, donning paper hats and singing for their tea. I sensed at once the reluctance of the group to be catapulted by their leader into second childhood. I realised we would only get through the ensuing mutual embarrassment were I to assume the role of the oldest among them, bravely attempting a walk in the woods but not entirely achieving it, being carried back to the sofa and managing a single bourbon chocolate biscuit.

Julian Bream now occupies my birth-place

Brave I was seen to be, to what might prove the end, by warding off a suspected attack of angina by swallowing an aspirin. I assured all that it was the merest touch of indigestion, begged them to tuck into the crumpets and cheerfully accepted their departure an hour earlier than was intended.

"Thank goodness we were here to help," they reiterated with the utmost cheer and composure. I had given them a renewed sense of responsibility and something to discuss on their way home.

3
Eating, Drinking, Etcetering

Are there petits fours *with the coffee?*

3
EATING,
DRINKING,
ETCETERING . . .

> *"I am very grateful to old age because it has increased my*
> *desire for conversation and lessened my desire for food*
> *and drink."*
>
> CICERO

O N THIS occasion I take exception to Cicero – actually on many occasions I take exception to Cicero. I am not well read. Indeed I hardly read at all. An early struggle with Latin and Greek ended in total defeat and a year abroad at the age of sixteen to recuperate. I have avoided the classics up to now – it doesn't really help in my case to know that others have had loftier opinions and expressed them better than I can, some two thousand years later. Besides, Cicero was a mere sixty-two when he wrote on the Pleasures of Age. To give it greater verisimilitude he pretended his friend Cato, eighty-four at the time, was the true author.

I have not noticed a lessened desire for food and drink.

"He seems to have gone off his food." A cat, a canary, a grandfather – it is a bad sign. Nowadays, however, there is an

outcry against the old-fashioned child-guardian who encouraged a clean plate. The world has gone mad about being
overweight. Diets, health farms, exercise and surgery all play
their part to persuade us that to be thin is to be healthy. No
one, I remind you, has ever seen a calorie. On the whole the
stout are happier, although in America women sometimes
grow to enormous proportions, and one wonders how they
manage on a plane, in the lavatory, making love. They have
obviously gone too far and must find it impossible shopping
for clothes. As far as clothes are concerned I have lived to enjoy
a revolution. Men of my size were once referred to as 'Out-
size'. How very unimaginative. Now we are King Size, Tall
and Proud, Cheerful Giants – there is quite a choice.

We are dealing now with the pleasure of eating. The excitement of taste, the scent of curry, the perfume of garlic, the
anticipatory chuckle of one's nose outside a coffee shop or a
bakery, the aroma of sausages and bacon and eggs. Alas, I no
longer eat breakfast at home, but staying in a hotel where the
price is often included I indulge. The only form I have ever
enjoyed filling (besides my own) is the one you hang outside
the bedroom door. Cereal with fresh fruit, choice of Canadian
bacon with two eggs (any style), corn-beef hash, kippers
individually smoked in pairs, which never, however, match in
taste. Wondering why, I once wrote to *The Times*. My reward
was a whole case from the Smoked Haddock Board. In my
youth there was a tradition of coming down to breakfast with
kidney, kedgeree, cold pheasant and sausages in chafing dishes
on the sideboard. On waking one was expected to be healthy
and wealthy and indeed hungry. One rang for fresh toast and
tea and discussed the prospects for hunting, shooting and
fishing. Actually, I wasn't ever exactly in that league but
somehow I know all about it. I am not quite so happy about
helping myself in hotels where the butter and cream are
packaged, the orange juice is served in medicine glasses and the
toast, long since popped, is tired. I then must carry the tray the

long march back to my table and find myself enviously glancing at my neighbours and cursing myself that I failed to find the yoghurt or the pancakes.

In America, breakfast is the best meal of the day. The drugstore counter, the little hot-cakes or waffles with maple syrup, the fried eggs easy on an English muffin, the hash brown potatoes, the constantly refilled coffee mug – even though the coffee has grown worse and worse over the years, the supply is endless and that aspect still causes pleasure.

Of course there is a price to be paid for over-eating, even at breakfast. A price which has nothing to do with age. I was a bilious child. Once lying on the sofa with one of my too frequent sick headaches my mother called the doctor who sketched two circles of disproportionate size on the otherwise clean tablecloth.

"This one here," he indicated the smaller one, "is the size of your stomach, young man, and here," he sought to increase the size of the other, "is what you persist in stuffing it with."

It was Mother who objected to the slight. I was feeling too ill to protest. He had used an indelible pen to sketch his outlandish theory and was never again consulted by either of us. The pain passed but the hurt to my feelings remains after seventy-four years.

Luncheon, despite a slight diminishment of appetite, perhaps due to breakfast, remains for us seniors the most serious meal of the day. The later generations seem too often nowadays to have trivialised it – unless they have an expense account or are domiciled abroad. There is no more heart-warming sight than the Frenchman on his bicycle bringing home the bread attached to his carrier or better still steering his vehicle with one hand while the loaves, tucked under his armpit, are clutched firmly with the other. The French are an unsteady

race, especially on wheels, and instead of the school run they
have the bread run – a much more satisfactory arrangement.

At my advanced age, I find great pleasure in presiding over a
cooking programme in New York. Celebrities are supposed
to call in at my kitchen and cook their favourite dish. Corn
bread with molasses, nasturtium leaves salted in garlic butter,
soul food and hop-scotch bread puddings. I stand by adding
lemon or egg-white to their taste. Afterwards we sit down and
eat and they tell me casually of a book which is about to be
published, or of a series of concerts to be played. I am devoted
to cooking programmes although mine is the only one from
which I receive cash as well as guidance.

How seldom do things go wrong in television kitchens.
They beat the batter, slurp the wine, stuff the partridge and all
is ready in a trice. The secret of cooking is courage and
washing-up as you go along, but television chefs don't have to
bother. Every taste is succulent. Not so, of course, for the food
writers, of whom I was one for a spell. I tried to steer away
from the perpetual disappointment over the *crème brûlée*. I
forebore to mention that my wife chose the *crevettes au Port
Merion*, or how much the bill came to. Still it is reassuring to
note how much money I was paid.

I found it more rewarding to talk to the chefs. Theirs is a
tough trade. It takes three hours to prepare the mackerel and
then the whole thing is wolfed down in the same number of
minutes.

A friend of mine, on retiring from the teaching profession,
donned a pinny, acquired a library of exotic cookery books
and has spent many a happy day in the kitchen stuffing the
poussin and whipping the pavlova. He has come in a few short
years from a man who could just spread the paste on the toast
to one of the finest amateur chefs in Oxfordshire. Each year he
invites a master chef or two to stay.

"I don't let them mess about," he told me, "just cook the
dishes they are famous for. Do you know what distinguishes

the amateurs from the professionals? The latter keep their hats on and turn the gas full up."

I don't cook myself: I am far too adventurous. It is the last daring addition of the tinned gooseberries, contrary to the guidebook's instructions, that ruins my efforts.

The pleasure of afternoon tea is an abiding experience for the senior citizen, especially when someone else has cut the cucumber sandwiches, baked the scones, heated the crumpets, whipped the cream and opened the pot of strawberry jam, sliced the Dundee and arranged the chocolate biscuits. Every year there is a special feast prepared by my already mentioned friend in Oxford. We all bring cameras to record the table before the crackers are pulled and decorations disturbed by those over-reaching for mince pies and flap-jacks.

For many of us nowadays dinner has become supper, partly because we sleep better afterwards and partly because after breakfast, luncheon and tea we are no longer hungry.

"Just a boiled egg," I tell my wife, "two perhaps with a *soupçon* of pâté and what's left of the treacle tart."

I tell you what does seem to have gone from life at any rate: fish paste.

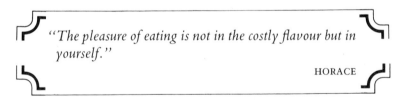

"The pleasure of eating is not in the costly flavour but in yourself."

HORACE

What could Horace have meant? I haven't, of course, been asked out to the tables of the rich as often as some. The nature of my trade, nocturnally on stage, debarred me from accepting a great many invitations – well, a few anyway. When I did accept I did not always enjoy myself. A plethora of silver kept one on the quiver as to which fork to pick up next. I dreaded the dish proffered by a footman of which I was the first to partake. I have been known to disregard the cutlet and confine myself to the aspic. Sometimes my hostess was as unpredictable as my table manners. What was I to make of Dorothy Paget, who, after my performance, would begin hers in the Rolls-Royce which was to take us to dine? On occasion, for an hour or so at a time, we would be confined to her motor, anchored outside her front door while the caviar warmed and the goose waned and she expounded her theories of horse-breeding.

Then too there was the night she took me to the Café de Paris to hear Noël Coward, who, to my certain knowledge, had concluded his season a month earlier. I was prepared for her disappointment when she summoned the Maître and asked if he could persuade Mr Coward to postpone his performance for half an hour or so.

"I do not care to be sung to while I am eating," Miss Paget explained. She was a diabetic with a prodigious appetite.

"That will be easy, Miss Paget," the head waiter replied, "Mr Coward is no longer with us."

"Whom have you got?" she asked, and on being informed who was to take his place opined that as she had never heard of him his fee should be placed on her bill and his services dispensed with. She was reminded that she was by no means the sole patron of the restaurant.

"Well," she commanded, "tell him to delay until I have finished the lobster and we'll be off."

There was Mrs Loder, too, who ordered a sumptuous feast at the Cannes Casino, but who delayed entering the restaurant while she waited for seventeen to turn up at the roulette wheel on which she customarily staked the maximum allowed in the Salle Privée.

Then there was the Christmas dinner at Duveen's which went on for several hours while the guests feasted and our host pecked assiduously at a small portion of scrambled egg – whether this behaviour was as a reproof to the rest of us or some sort of dietary constriction I never discovered.

Eating, like swimming, is one of the last great exercises in which the truly aged indulge. I seldom pass a restaurant or cease to wonder at the almost complete disappearance (except outside the least inviting of public houses) of the traditional announcement of joint and two veg. I browse, however, happily among the descriptions of individually prepared duckling from our own pond with specially imported Chinese fig stuffing and carefully selected garden-fresh sea-kale. This they proclaim is the favourite dish of Manchurian warriors. Then there is the home-cooked apple-pie prepared from a secret recipe left us by Grandma. Or what about a warm salad of bacon rind served on a tantalising bed of individually buttered parsnips with forced celery. And oh, the puddings – just to stand and read about white and black chocolate ice-cream topped with cream and raspberry *coulis*. How menus have changed. Alas, it is only ten-thirty in the morning and goodness knows why I am feeling so peckish in Saffron Walden. But the mere contemplation of the choice is pleasure in itself.

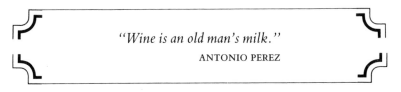

"Wine is an old man's milk."
ANTONIO PEREZ

Wine, although an undoubted pleasure, remains a mystery to me.

"It has as yet a rather thin nose but its colour is surprisingly bold for an '85 Medoc."

"Slightly lacking in bramble but with a reasonable after-taste of walnut and mercifully short of raspberry, it has deceived finer palates than mine in its provenance which is of course the small vineyard of Haut St Juste just left of the garage as one motors past Lyons on the road to Château Lafonde."

"A wine which justifies laying down at least until the '95s

with only a slight risk that it might shed its essential peat impression. A fine buy at seventeen pounds a bottle but alas only in limited supply."

Thus do the experts tease us with their own superior wisdom. I have always been a dunce where wine is concerned and a bit of a coward when ordering a bottle in a restaurant or selecting from the shelves of a supermarket. I go for the medium price range and hope people will accept me as a connoisseur. In truth I know nothing but refuse to be hyped by the Beaujolais Nouveau. I remember the first time I was allowed a glass of Graves, freely diluted with soda water. The Gare du Nord just after the First World War. In those days the mixture was labelled hock and seltzer, now it is called a spritzer.

Just as I don't see properly out of one eye, I have sensory deprivation if I am ever tempted to roll the stuff round behind my gums and spit it out. What pleasure can there be in such a pastime? I find it difficult to imagine. Besides, I often choke.

If I ever learned anything at all about wine it should have been when I was acting at the Festival Theatre, Cambridge. There was never another quite like it and certainly no one I ever met since resembled the proprietor, Terence Gray, who was the son of the local MP and whose family residence was called Gog and Magog. He produced about eight plays each term, amongst which Latin comedies by Terence and Greek dramas by Euripides featured prominently. But by far his most ambitious project was his wine list that accompanied the food which graced the restaurant he ran on the same site. Each term he featured what were guaranteed to be the last six bottles extant of a renowned claret. These he priced at thirty pounds to entice the local young bloods and the supply was apparently inexhaustible. Eventually he retired to a vineyard in the South of France and became one of those immensely courteous and refined wine-growers who live to an incredible old age hunting the wild boar and dressing for dinner.

To be an eye, nose and throat specialist in such élitist

circumstances is, alas, only the privilege of the few, but the possession of a supply of yeast and the discovery of a small plantation of elderberries provides a hobby and excitement for senior citizens. All that is required is a book of instructions, a visit to the local chemist and the temporary use of the bathroom and the airing cupboard. The amateur who commences with the mulling of the claret or the bottling of the sloe gin becomes, if his inclinations permit, the uprooter of the rhubarb and the plucker of the dandelions. Perhaps he even becomes the alchemist who transforms the humble potato into vodka. The singular triumph of the sommelier's acknowledgment that the wine is indeed corked, is not available at a neighbour's table when protesting the after-taste of his parsnip wine. He is almost certain to defend it with another bottle.

> *"Some sigh for this and that;*
> *My wishes don't go far;*
> *The world may wag at will,*
> *So I have my cigar."*
> THOMAS HOOD

> *"A woman is only a woman, but a good cigar is a Smoke."*
> RUDYARD KIPLING

Following the food and the wine, what greater pleasure than a cigar? Cigars, certainly the more expensive ones, arrive beautifully wrapped. Or more precisely, packaged. They are protected from the humdrum world by boxes made of cedar, and sold, no one quite knows why, in multiples of twenty-five, so that in the boxes I buy (or better yet someone gives me) there is a sort of square wooden dummy for which sadly I have never found a use. The empty box itself can, after the contents have gone up in smoke, be used on seaside holidays to attach sea shells. Others more imaginative than I juggle them on the music-hall stages. Nothing in the world is presented with more confidence – from the customs stamp on the lid to the small tack which secures it and the insignia on the inside announcing the number and description of the cabinet selection. Each one is rolled on the naked thigh of some señorita of surpassing elegance and beauty. For those like myself this all provides the last remaining link with ostentatious extravagance.

Cigars are the trademark of the professional survivor. Churchill, Korda, Grade, Burns – all puffed and chewed on them. Winston's celebrated V-sign was not originally a symbol of victory to come, but a cry for help when he had incautiously dropped his Havana on the carpet and desired someone to get down on his hands and knees to retrieve it. As he observed an aide in crouching submission, inspiration struck.

There are lunatics among us who do not appreciate the aroma. There are women who cough ostentatiously or wave racecards vigorously when seated beside one. Once in a remote airfield while making a picture, a runner was dispatched from the star to beg me to refrain from puffing within a distance of at least a quarter of a mile, as he was allergic to the scent and dreaded the onslaught of pneumonia. I calculated a bout in his case would ensure an extra week's work and lit up happily. Pneumonia did not ensue and we finished the picture on time.

"I suffer from age, heart trouble, arthritis, kidney failure and liver fatigue," I told him later. "You merely from hypochondria – so shut up."

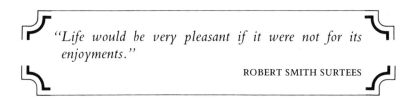

"Life would be very pleasant if it were not for its enjoyments."

ROBERT SMITH SURTEES

Either you enjoy parties or you don't. It is unlikely that age will influence your attitude. I was a party-marty in childhood. I was the last to be picked for a team of dumb crambo. When I got to the age when one was expected to dance, life (or at any rate Christmas holidays), was a sustained nightmare. Not that I was asked to a great many parties after a time. I was an uncouth, uncoordinated child who simply couldn't do better when I tried. It was almost as bad in the summer with the tennis. I was almost a total reject.

Perplexed by my own inability to jog around a dance floor I once attended the school of a Miss Ruby Peeler who guaranteed results. After three lessons Miss Peeler herself took charge. Briefly.

"We have a rule here," she told me, "never to despair and give up a pupil. You have convinced me to make an exception. I shall of course refund. Your task henceforth at dances will be to fetch the lemonade."

It was for me a life sentence.

But, for many, dancing remains an abiding pleasure and remarkably good exercise. However serious the mien, disciplined the posture, slow the progress, the correctness of the hold on one's partner's anatomy signals the contentment of those who have won the battle of life and are still prepared to salute their partner at the conclusion of the British Grenadiers.

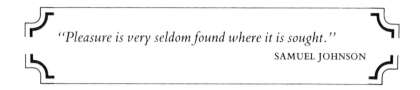

But what of other parties? Cocktail? I suppose one was always hoping to glimpse a stranger across a crowded room. I read a book that advised you always to have your back against a wall – preferably two walls. The theory was that that way one commanded the battle. I found the advice totally useless. Even in those days I could never place a face. Seen any of the old gang? Are you still living in the same house? Business still good? I fished and fished, casting flies where no trout surfaced. False confidence always betrayed.

"How is your husband? Did you bring him?" I ask.

"No, you came to his funeral last August."

Nowadays my hearing-aid doesn't help. Only when people tell me how well I am looking I no longer bridle. I realise they too have no idea to whom they speak.

The captain of a cruise ship hosts a cocktail party yet never falters over an introduction. In the event of disaster one is sure he will still be bobbing up in the waves, still introducing the drowning.

The one who sinks at a book party is invariably the author. The publishers expect him to sign copies. He may even expect to do so himself. Once at a function in Richmond, Virginia, which was held in a department store, I pursued a prospective quarry into the neighbouring toilet accessories.

"I am here with my husband," the lady informed me.

Rape was not on my mind, but she gave me an idea. I attacked the undisturbed pile of my work and wrote in each of them a declaration of passionate love – occasionally recalling the time and place of our night of ecstasy. These, at any rate, I told myself, shall not be returned to the publisher.

"There is no greater nor keener pleasure than that of bodily love – and none which is more irrational."

PLATO

"All men lie when they are asked about their adventures in amour."

H. L. MENCKEN

Or as Cicero puts it – "let sensuality be present and a good life becomes impossible". Is it a pleasure to enjoy with Plato the release of a man chained most of his life to the clutches of a madman? There are men, of course, who have procreated at eighty, who find pleasure in sex long after their ninetieth birthday and who continue potency in remote regions of Nepal and *The Guinness Book of Records*. This is beyond most of us, and – because I myself have no first-hand knowledge of such phenomena – the pleasure of sex for the aged is not included in this volume.

I am furthermore of the opinion that this is one pleasure – in either youth or age – which is better experienced than discussed.

4
Looking Back and Planning Ahead

I don't see why time should wait for no man

4
LOOKING BACK AND PLANNING AHEAD . . .

"I love everything that's old; old friends, old times, old manners, old books, old wines."

OLIVER GOLDSMITH

NOSTALGIA IS one of the great abiding pleasures. Here memory is at its most benign. Happy hours can be passed in the contemplation of the lady who sold balloons outside the gates of Kensington Gardens, the paper used by Mr Selfridge to line his chocolate boxes which could be ripped off after the fondants were consumed to simulate the firing of a Maxim gun. The straw outside the houses of the dying; the days when shopping at Harrods meant remaining in Grandmother's brougham while Mr Burbage detached himself from the fish counter and, raising his straw hat, prepared to write down the order. Customers waited upon indeed. Once I remember being decanted from an ambulance on a stretcher and experiencing the fascinated countenances of the spectators, and later riding along the Folkestone Leas in a bath chair with glass shutters to open and close at will and two attendants – one to push and one to pull. It was magic for a child all ready to spend a lifetime showing off. I remember with pleasure my first performance as a Chinaman at my kindergarten with a pigtail sewn into the lining of the hat and also remember with equal pleasure how, sixty years later, I tried to stop James Mason from attaching his with spirit-gum to the nape of his neck so as to avoid the inevitable skin rash, when he played a Chinaman in *Genghis Khan*. It was unavailing advice as it turned out. He insisted upon doing it properly. A rash performer.

At seven I was the definitive Father Christmas in the late Canon Elliot's Christmas pantomime in the Grand Hotel. I was in love – not only with my performance, but also with a girl called Rose. However, my childhood lust was unrequited. Learning that she was fond of riding I was always inciting my parents to take me to gymkhanas until the morning I was woken by the sound of jangling reins under my window and glimpsed my father awaiting me on a mettlesome steed and manipulating a pony on a leading rein. It took me a while to prove myself an unwilling horse boy.

The contemplation of servants surely comes into the nostalgia class. How different those days were when one was occupied 'keeping servants in their place' rather in the manner of the lady to whom I lost my passion in Majorca. It begins in the nursery, if one was that sort of child, and I was. Nannie Bucher (could that really have been her name?) saved my life with the aid of brandy and then emigrated to Detroit. I always planned to visit. "What was I really like as a baby, Nannie?"

Grandmother came to visit when Nannie was in charge. Inspected my sister and me through lorgnettes. Whatever happened to lorgnettes?

"The girl's all right, but the boy's an idiot."

I don't think she lived long enough for me to prove her mistaken. We were taken to say goodbye when she was dying in a great bed. Hanging behind her on the wall was an embroidered bell ribbon. She tugged it almost as soon as we had kissed her and Hinchley ushered us out. Later, and for reasons never explained, we inherited Hinchley, but not for long. I imagine it was Father's idea that she should join the household. She was the nearest he ever came to a butler. Hinchley was a parlourmaid. It was in the days when Father's cavalry helmet, converted into a biscuit tin, plumes and all, adorned the hall table along with a mysterious silver box attached to a bell. This was all that remained of his regimental trophies and they joined the silver salver for visiting cards – the equivalent of today's junk mail. They too often came through the letter-box unbidden. Coachmen went round delivering them while the occupants of the brougham stayed put.

Father was wont in later years to pine for Hinchley, who had a way with his trousers. Mother pined for the silver canteen which Father had pawned. I don't think Hinchley pined for any of us. It must have been a relief for her when we could no longer afford staff in the plural.

For most of her life Mother employed at least one cook-housekeeper and what my father referred to as a *Bonne à Tout Faire*. *Bonne* skipped two generations and still keeping her identity foreign became an *au pair*. None of Mother's *au pairs* were remotely foreign and her attitude to them was distinctly formal. There were recognisable periods when their attendance was not demanded: usually one afternoon a week. At an early age she instilled in me the maxim that one should never on any account watch them at their mealtimes.

While the servants served, Mother read everything that Berta Ruck published. When she had finished the latest work she would close the book thoughtfully and hurl it across the room.

"Why?" I once asked.

"Trying for the waste-paper basket," she replied. "The hours I waste on that woman!"

Strictly speaking it wasn't Mother's book at all but belonged to Boots' Lending Library. Ah nostalgia! I do miss Boots and the hooks in the binding to which one attached the shield of membership. If, like Mother and me, you mostly read rubbish, in her case romantic novels and in mine detective stories, there is still Harrods, one supposes. But then I live in the country. Libraries do remain a pleasure for the aged. They remain warm and welcoming when one can think of nowhere else to go.

The library committee at Harrods wrote a personal letter of condolence to a widow of my acquaintance. "This is the first time we have done such a thing," was the gist of it, "but, as you know, Sir George was in every day."

The widow was dumbfounded. Every day? At Harrods Library? But for a number of years she had dutifully ferried him to and from his office in the City. Not once had he mentioned Harrods. Not once had she picked him up there.

"If only he had told me how he spent the day," she observed, "it would have saved pounds in petrol."

"That which is bitter to endure may be sweet to remember."
THOMAS FULLER

"Oft in the stilly night,
Ere Slumber's chain has bound me,
Fond Memory brings the light
Of other days around me;
The smiles, the tears,
Of boyhood's years,
The words of love then spoken;
THOMAS MOORE

Sir Frederick Pollock was Editor-in-Chief of the Law Reports until he reached the age of ninety-one. A few years before his retirement, however, he paused at the age of eighty-eight to write: *For my Grandson: Remembrances of an Ancient Victorian.*

Just a little light reading

Instant recognisability is not necessary for the compilation of memoirs. They may be written for publication, but perhaps for family perusal, perhaps merely for one's own amusement. Although, I hear there is a growing industry in the sale of tape recorders as children are encouraged to solicit the memories of grandparents for future reference. Family-tree hunting is not only big business but a growing cottage industry.

Alexander Murison even found time to break off in his translation of the *Iliad* to write his *Memoirs of 88 Years*. Sir Edward George Clarke prematurely wrote *The Story of My Life* when he was seventy-seven. Well, he couldn't have known he was going to live to be ninety. However, he was obviously a man who believed in planning ahead. He wrote a long obituary of himself for *The Times* and sent it along to the editor explaining that he felt the obituary of a man who had reached a certain age should undoubtedly be written by himself. When the time came the obituary was duly published. How nice to be in charge of one's own reputation.

Even royalty is not above the practice. Princess Marie Louise was eighty-four when she published her memoirs, *My Memories of Six Reigns*, and she had the added pleasure of selling over forty thousand copies in a couple of months. However, it is not in commercialism that the pleasure necessarily resides. That could be considered a bonus. The pleasure is in conjuring up the past – and amending it when the spirit takes one – that is so satisfying.

> "A man's memory may almost become the art of his continually varying and misrepresenting his past according to his interests in the present."
>
> GEORGE SANTAYANA

I could not take issue with a single sentence, a tiny observation, in *Footprints in Malaya*, which Sir Frank Swettenham, the colonial administrator, published when he was ninety-one – our paths were disparate. There are, however, now available to me the memoirs of my contemporaries. Surely, I say as I read the reminiscences of an aged thespian, the Wolverhampton Theatre was on the Station Road and not the High Street. Did Tyrone Guthrie really say that to Edith Evans? I was there and I don't recall the conversation. So many events are documented and conversations recorded with which I would take issue. There is much pleasure to be taken in contemplating the superiority of my memory – or not, as the case may be.

I would highly recommend the immediate taking-up of pen to those who, on the pleasant side of retirement, find themselves with a few hours to spare to record their life and experiences. For the family? For posterity? For the local gazetteer? No, for the sheer pleasure of invention.

There is a school of faith which brings solace to some of the old, and the young for that matter, on the basis that at the moment of death or at least as soon as the rather complicated procedure has been accomplished, they will be reunited with their relatives and loved ones. Cicero believed in life after death and looked forward to grand reunion parties with the dear departed. Would I wish to meet up with my family, of which I suppose I am now the sole survivor? My mother and father and all those aunts? What sort of welcoming party would they provide? What would they have planned? Are they at this moment already planning some sort of celestial picnic? Would I be embarrassed or bored, I wonder? Would memory return so that I could identify each one? I do find it a shade disquieting that I can still conjure them up without effort whereas I am at a loss to recognise friends who appear on my television screen. Evelyn, Edith, Betty, Sophie, Lily, Connie, Mardi, Gracie, Marjorie, and the boys, Dolph, Frank, Ernest, Basil, Edgar, Reggie. Are they and all the others lying in wait? Could I be wrong as I so often am? I would, I suppose, feel happier meeting old friends – but only just.

On the other hand, Cicero, hedging his bets as is so often his wont, says he cannot dismiss entirely the belief held by others that there is no life after death and concludes that if we are not going to become immortal it is still acceptable for a man to come to his end at the proper time. When Life's last act becomes wearisome it is time to go. Such spiritual considerations seldom exercise my brain. Ever since I consulted – no, consult is not the word. Ever since I was received by an internationally acclaimed guru at three in the morning on a housing estate in Delhi I have accepted her lightning diagnosis of my spiritual ambitions.

"You are not," she told me, "ever to worry about why you are here or what you are supposed to be doing on earth. Such matters should never, I repeat, never concern you."

Once I asked Graham Greene to tell me his most urgent wish. To die in the state of grace was all he asked.

The question came up recently on television.

"I would like," a recent Lord Chancellor replied, "to make my peace with God."

How, I wondered, did he propose to go about it? How had the war started? If he had at one time taken on God how had he, as a devout Churchman, hoped to win the battle, let alone the war?

I personally have no such quarrel. I am convinced the

With Morecambe and Wise, but where were we?

Almighty doesn't know I am here. I certainly don't wish to continue to be myself for an unspecified eternity. When one is eighty it is natural that one should have grown tired of one's self. But a man who is tired of himself is not, to paraphrase Johnson, necessarily tired of life.

One of the many blessings of age is the gradual slackening of concentration. What might happen one asks oneself if babies were no longer born? Or if it was suddenly apparent that all who lived to their seventieth birthday were to die at that age? As one considers the implications one is suddenly aware that the brain has switched its attention to a cursory examination of fish-hooks. Occasionally, as with dreams, an effort brings about a reversal of the thought process but usually one is left with the fish-hook which as a boy cut deep into my thumb when fishing from the quay in Dieppe. I was an extravagantly clumsy child at school. I could never draw a box let alone make one. In the dormitory there were rings fastened to a beam. Juniors were expected to do pull-ups or get beaten. Nowadays I sometimes have difficulty doing up a button but I am no longer beaten for failing. The sheer pleasure . . .

Where was I? Oh, yes, death and beyond. My own father was always exploring graveyards for a possible site. He very much favoured cedar trees.

"Just about here, dear," and putting one shoe behind the other he would pace out seven feet. He never stipulated the width. In the end we cremated him.

In the days of my grandmother there was much more ground space. A family tomb was enclosed by railings of which I was once rather proud. Chalfont St Giles – the name resounds – but graves, however high-sounding, are not possessions. Nor are trees for that matter, until they fall on someone else's greenhouse.

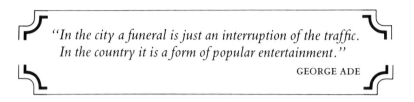

*"In the city a funeral is just an interruption of the traffic.
In the country it is a form of popular entertainment."*

GEORGE ADE

Planning one's funeral can be an endless source of pleasure.
Large or small? By invitation or not? I do not know why the
Church dwells, I often feel, with satisfaction, on the final
admonition in the burial service that it is certain we can take
nothing into the next world. As we know so little about the
conditions which will prevail I have left instructions that my
credit cards should be buried alongside myself.

It is only natural that from time to time the aged should
contemplate the final disposal and wish to have a hand in the
arrangements. Queen Victoria for instance remained the Mis-
tress of the Proceedings even to the ordering of the most
minute details and instructions as to what relics should be
placed in her coffin and by whom. At the other end of the scale
there is a hope that the funeral service should be as brief and
economical as possible and should on no account be followed
by a memorial service or what is called nowadays, with a hint
of ambiguity, a Service of Thanksgiving.

If ever there occurred a hitch at a burying it was always
presumed it would add to the amusement and pleasure of the
deceased watching from afar or possibly just overhead. No
one, however, could really bring themselves to believe that
George V was chuckling or indeed chuffed when some piece of
regalia was displaced as the cortège took a corner a shade too
sharply.

Just back from the Requiem for an old friend, I found myself
wondering how he would fare in the next world if the prayers
of the congregation were answered and he was to meet
Abraham and be conducted by the saints into the presence of
the Almighty at the earliest possible moment. Would there be

the inevitable delays of officialdom or would there be no such problems in the miraculous manipulations of time everlasting? Above all, how would the initial interview go? He was a rather shy man, at least for a bookmaker, with impeccable manners. I was fantasising on his subsequent reassurance by Abraham.

"No, no, the Almighty took to you at once. He doesn't always shake hands. And you notice God stood when you took your leave. Most satisfactory the whole interview and now there is just the question of kitting you out with a really good quality pair of wings. You'll find they do take a little time to get used to."

Meanwhile back to memorial services of which members of my own profession are so extravagantly fond and so freely available to strum on a harp, sing the occasional aria or read from the deceased's favourite passage from *Alice in Wonderland*. There is also of course the eulogy in which a colleague gossips informally about the deceased and reveals his fondness not only for his public but also for the helter-skelter of life backstage and his lifelong passions for Guinness and cold roast beef. And how reassured he would be at the size of the house. It is this last anxiety that prevents most of us holding the thanksgiving ceremony during our lifetime – that, of course, and the fear that the date of our departure might clash with an ex-ambassador and due to lack of space upset the very natural desire for a really prominent obituary in the columns of *The Times*.

The last request of Chinese martial artist Ku Lung was to be buried with two hundred bottles of cognac. His relatives obliged but could only fit forty-eight bottles of Hennessy XO into the casket.

The Vikings believed that people should be buried with useful things so the chieftain got interred in a longship. It seems even lesser corpses were given wild apples to nibble on the voyage to the land of the dead.

Boats also figured in the burial rites of the Egyptians. Now the Egyptians – they really knew how to plan for death. Rameses II was over ninety when he died around 1237 BC. He had reigned over a not easy country for sixty-seven years. He had five wives and more than a hundred children but he still set aside time to make sure everything would be to his liking when the end came. And it worked. His mummy was preserved for 3,000 years. Of course, the funeral ceremonies included magical rites to ensure that the mummy would not only endure but would also enjoy eternal life. The tomb was full of food and drink. Also, he managed to set aside some money to maintain a priest whose occupation was making sure the tomb was regularly restocked with comestibles. The priest presumably also took on the task of disposing of the rotting ones, as well as keeping to himself the fact that the model boat placed in the tomb for the soul to sail on the pilgrimage to the sacred city of Osiris, Abydos, was still firmly at anchor.

Now the Etruscans were mainly aesthetic in their choice of items to be buried with them. They opted for jewellery and well-crafted pieces of pottery. But their send-offs were not noted for religious solemnity. Taking a leaf from the Greeks, they brought the concept of funeral games to a heady excitement. Not for them the comparative understatement of an Irish wake or a Jewish *shiva* or a C of E "come back from the cemetery for a glass of sherry". There was wrestling and boxing, as the Greeks had had beforehand, but they added another dimension. Gladiators fought to the death. This was, I suppose, sensible. It meant there would soon be an excuse for another party.

What further should I request be placed beside me for the final journey? My life is filled with possessions – not of value unfortunately but those countless inanimate objects that seem to challenge one to discard them. Am I the only person who never throws away hearing-aid batteries? In a box on my dressing-table lie hundreds – all spent. I read once that you should never, never put them on the fire or leave them lying around for children to swallow. I have always dreaded the moment I should inadvertently pop one in my mouth in the absent-minded belief that it was a pill.

There can be less excuse surely for the presence of a Key to the City of New Orleans, or a wooden dog that used to pop out its tongue and swallow a dime, or Dracula who, on pressing a button, blushed and dropped his trousers. All, alas, are no longer in working order.

Then there are a dozen or so small leather cases which once held cuff-links or evening-dress studs or even tie-pins. Among the boxes lie lighters which no longer flame, watches that no longer tick and single cuff-links which refuse to swivel. Why do I not discard them? Would they be of more use to me in the next world than they are in this? No. I shall stick to my plan – American Express, Diners, Visa – assorted plastic should see me through to eternity and I won't be getting the bills, having wisely not completed the change-of-address form.

5
Daily Doing

Where are my glasses?

5
DAILY
DOING . . .

> "Lord of himself, though not of lands;
> And having nothing, yet hath all."
> SIR HENRY WOOTON

> "Praise those that will times past, I joy to see
> Myself now live: this age best pleaseth me."
> ROBERT HERRICK

To PLEASE oneself – such bliss. To rise when one likes, to sleep when one desires – and all the myriad pleasures of the time in between. It could be said, however, that George Bidder, the noted marine biologist, took this to extremes. Becoming nocturnal as he grew older he took to rising not before teatime and spending the night in work. So adamant was he at adhering to this, his preferred schedule, and so much did the 'normal' world intervene that he bought himself a hotel in Naples to ensure that the more conventional timetables of others did not interfere with him. There he lived happily into his nineties, studying sponges.

I myself often wake with the intention of getting up early. Early for me that is. I am aware that the Monarch herself is an early riser, along with the postman and the 'paper-motorist' and whole flights of early birds with business in the city. But for myself, nine is about the time I open my eyes gratefully on a new day and resolve to get something done say by eleven.

Then my wife brings up the coffee and I go down for the papers and an hour slips by while I read how exceptionally idle has been the rest of mankind.

Good heavens, a spotted buzzard, a species not seen in Britain for twelve years has suddenly appeared near a haystack in the Lake District and a hundred amateur ornithologists are in hot pursuit. Trains are reported turning away second-class passengers to Ullswater; the roads are blocked and conservationists have been issued with small arms.

A man queues outside Harrods for a week waiting to buy a diamond watch which has been reduced by a hundred-thousand pounds. He is still there, and I am still in bed.

There is a lot still to be done, I remind myself. There are the taps to be turned on for the bath, the oil uncorked for the bubbles, the face still to be explored for the possibility of skipping the shave. Yet here I am still with the newspapers, scavenging amongst the deaths in case I have missed someone. Often the names are familiar but carry a suspect provenance.

REED – Basil Thomas, after a long illness, borne with great dignity.

MILNE – Lady Sashia, after suffering bravely endured.

We *Times* readers are so often exceptional in our manifest courage. It is strange how no one ever seems to succumb with sudden terror in Dorking.

After the deaths I must peruse the birthdays. A famous journalist has complained that his birthday went unnoticed by *The Times*. It is a rule with me that unless I know personally at least one of those mentioned, I postpone even further getting out of bed. The day does not augur well and I hesitate to commence it a moment earlier than I need. I know that getting up isn't really the beginning any more than getting into bed marks the end, but for me bed is another country in a different time zone. Any excuse to travel is seized upon. At the first sign of a cold I am off for the Lemsip, the hot-water bottle and pleasurable snuffles between the sheets.

"I don't," I explain, "want the grandchildren to catch anything but if one of them felt strong enough they might care to tie their handkerchief over nose and mouth and lug upstairs the portable television and if it is not too much trouble, a honey sandwich with my tea. You know what they say, stuff a cold and starve a fever and I'm pretty sure I'm not running a temperature yet."

But now the coffee has grown cold and the papers are in total disarray. I could of course postpone the moment of rising indefinitely, if I was at all attracted by the crossword. Crosswords can occupy hours, if not days. I am indebted to *The Guinness Book of Records* for bringing to my attention the Fijian lady who wrote to *The Times* informing them she had finally completed a crossword which they had published thirty-four years previously. Obviously she had just been waiting for the time to concentrate properly.

To the bath. How sad that I get so little pleasure from my own bathroom. I think enviously of those sturdy contemporaries who still float plastic ducks under the taps and generally enjoy themselves for a quarter of an hour after breakfast, or sometimes before. For them it is a great pleasure in which they indulge at their leisure after many years of hurried showers on the way to somewhere else – marching to another's tune.

At school, once a week was considered sufficient. There was even one school that encouraged, nay decreed, cold baths. But then, of course, cold water was no stranger to my generation. There was no such thing as central heating; double-glazing would have been considered eccentric, almost lunatic. Ice on the water jugs was a way of life, mirrors steamed, but only with our breath.

Then after school was mercifully completed – or abandoned as in my case – there were the digs at which I stayed, as up and down the country I toured in plays. Money was tight and baths were often extra. How nervous one was of geysers. Landladies' bathrooms featured other toothbrushes and foreign flannels. Another person's letter which I am not meant to read always attracts; another person's toiletries repel.

My own bathroom sports a medicine cupboard. If the door is opened incautiously, unattractive aids to health fall from it. The purpose of each remedy is long since forgotten but sometimes, when restacking the shelves, I ponder over instructions. One every four hours if the symptoms persist . . . two night and morning . . . apply to affected surface . . . keep out of reach of children. But the date. Surely I was almost a child myself in those days.

Next to the shaving cream and the disposable razors on the shelf over the basin, three little bottles of pills reside. These are current. I am supposed to take one from each every morning and sometimes I do. My system must be thoroughly tired of them and so am I. Taking pills is not a pleasure of age, although luckily I have always been able to swallow. It is not a skill which has deserted me. Some of my family choke and demand water – not I. I remember when I was young and I swallowed a whole sugared almond. Mother panicked. So did I come to that. At the dentist I am still plagued by a desire to swallow anything the operator deposits momentarily on my tongue.

But back to the bathroom where others spend happy hours but, alas, not I. Turning on the hot water almost always displaces the plug and I suffer a slight scalding of my fingers replacing it. Christmas has brought me the bath essence. I have a variety – some bubbles. I have never believed those advertisements which state that after a foam bath something unexpected occurs. Stepping out I have never glimpsed an unknown admirer poised below in the garden. The most I ever catch sight of is a squirrel burrowing in the turf.

Lying in the opaque water I wonder if it is necessary to soap.

I get depressed – how soon even the sturdiest sponge disintegrates; with what frequency the soap slips from my grasp. When I wash my hair and dunk under to rinse out the last traces of shampoo I remind myself of Mr Smith drowning his victims by a swift hoist, then, clambering out cautiously, I submit to the tiresome process of drying.

Now I am back to square one and if I remember to do so I rescue the flannel, let out the water and begin to recover my equanimity with the thought that the whole absurd manoeuvre is over for another twenty-four hours.

How I envy others who find pleasure in taking a bath. How I envy them their rapture and how sad I am that fate decided I was not to be among them.

What definitely cannot be counted in any way a pleasure is the first occasion one is cast in one's bath. A sudden slackness of the muscles, an awkward position of the body supine and one is suddenly panicked into the realisation that help is required. The solution came to me in Australia after a month of showering and the abandonment of the bottle of bath oil. A new design is imperative. There I found a square bathtub. We live and can continue to do so when new designs are now perfected and can be installed. It is curious how slow has been man's realisation that the narrow standard tub, the steep-sided model, is no longer suited for the less agile. I don't pretend that this discovery alone made my latest visit to the upside-down continent as enjoyable as it was – but it certainly helped.

> *"A short letter to a friend is, in my opinion, an insult like that of a slight bow or cursory salutation – a proof of unwillingness to do much, even where there is a necessity of doing something."*
>
> SAMUEL JOHNSON

Old age gives me time to linger over the post. Bernard Shaw wrote on an average ten letters a day. I myself grew up in an age of correspondence. My mother's large family wrote to each other most days – sibling to sibling, niece to aunt, Mother to at least one child. Dutifully they exchanged impressions, described the weather and the scenery, itemised their likes and dislikes. To those, like myself, who never really manage to fill up the space on the back of a picture postcard, it might be thought that the absence of mail might present some sort of gap in my life. Not so. I average at least six letters each morning. It is true I am not exactly intimate with the senders but they all have two things in common. Most of them are fairly exalted in office. If they are not General Managers they are certainly Vice-Presidents or Chairpersons. Anyway they are manifestly caring, responsible people and all share a common concern: me. They all want to help by letting me in on what used to be known as the 'ground floor'. The first thought that comes to them while they are shaving is: "Why not let old Morley acquire one of our personalised pigskin travel card-cases, a collection of enamelled thimbles or even a selection of game ready for hanging?"

In order to find out what I really need a certain amount of research into my circumstances must obviously have taken place. They must know for instance that I have no alternative means of climbing stairs; that my loft is still a loft and not an alternative nursery. They must even know that my house is not one in which I can drop a feather and discover it will fall immediately to the floor. Rather it floats on in an eternal draught. I feel some of them worry about my state of mind.

"We mustn't," they tell each other, "just let old Morley sit there without some sort of project upon which to embark. We will send him the wine, of course, but let's first give him a token task. Let's ask him to recruit two other card-carrying members or find a friend to take out a subscription to *Horse and Hound*. Moreover we must encourage him to believe there is an urgency about the task. He must get cracking or the offer will end sooner than he thinks."

Task completed, I am told I will receive a case of half-a-dozen assorted sherry wines. Then I suppose it is expected that I will not drink myself to death before the post brings yet another opportunity to acquire an ornamental Egyptian scarab beetle.

The old do well to remember how high a priority they command in the caring thoughts of the investment brokers and insurance managers: the bullion dealers of this world. Although I seldom write letters, literally hundreds write to me each year, suggesting ways in which I can lead a happier, fuller existence. It would seem that the ink has hardly dried on the new scheme roughed out on a general manager's scribbling pad when the bell is touched, a secretary summoned and instructed to have the whole thing printed up in the form of a personal letter to old reliable Robert Morley.

"I really think," the GM murmurs, "this is what the old gentleman has been waiting for – a chance to participate in our Exceptional Circumstances Bonus Payments. In future he will be able to visit the circus secure in the knowledge that should a tiger break loose and bite off his arm he can claim a prodigious sum in damages, even though he was not wearing a coat at the time."

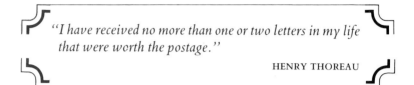

"I have received no more than one or two letters in my life that were worth the postage."

HENRY THOREAU

We oldies are fortunate in that it is a rare day indeed when our post does not include two or three unexpected opportunities. Invitations arrive to travel the world in search of adventure, to witness the exodus of giant eels anxious to add to their numbers by their mysterious, and often tragic, pilgrimage to the Sargasso Sea. We are offered the opportunity to establish once and for all the evidence of the survival of the Yeti, or to travel in the company of a 'Renowned International Authority' to the recently excavated site of the birthplace of Genghis Khan and the late Yul Brynner in Outer Mongolia.

We may well decide to postpone such excitement to a later year but, meanwhile, decisions are called for on whether to acquire treasures available nearer to home. How about starting to make a collection of teapots, plates or freshly minted medallions sponsored by the Royal Mint and Alkhair Investment and Development Ltd, the holding company of Art and Arts Ltd, based no further away than Cyprus? This last offer is currently on my desk. There is the customary acknowledgment that the offer is made in the name of Allah most mighty and most merciful. The prospectus points out that over the past fourteen centuries innumerable attempts have been made to portray the great events of the march of Islam and that now at last this has been achieved through an innovative method of expression – behold the Message Collection, consisting of thirteen beautifully minted commemorative gold medallions of which only three thousand of each set will be issued and, therefore, only possessed by very privileged people. And of course rather rich ones, as the first three medallions cost well over a thousand pounds and once I have embarked there will be no turning back until I have acquired the further ten. It is a pity that I cannot find the stamped addressed envelope in which remittance must be enclosed. At my age there are certain privileges that I must forgo – too much brandy and now too many gold medallions.

> *"It ought to be quite as natural and straightforward a matter for a labourer to take his pension from his parish, because he has deserved well of his parish, as for a man in higher rank to take his pension from his country, because he has deserved well of his country."*
>
> JOHN RUSKIN

Besides offers, the post occasionally contains rewards. I am very partial to pensions. In addition to one or two rather mysterious private schemes which I fondly imagine are now showing a profit, as I have managed to survive a respectable number of years since I first started paying in, there is my state pension which arrives every two or three months and the one from the United States as a reward for not arguing in the days when I was making pictures over there. Not many pictures it is true but then it is not a very large pension – yet always welcome. In the United Kingdom we all get the same from the State. I don't know why, but I always harbour a sense of resentment on the manner of the dole. Even the Christmas bonus is unaccompanied by 'Best Wishes'.

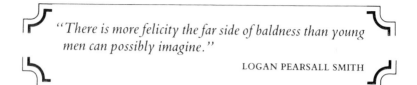

> *"There is more felicity the far side of baldness than young men can possibly imagine."*
>
> LOGAN PEARSALL SMITH

Sleep in the afternoon! Pleasure, and certainly nothing to be ashamed of. Lions all do it after a kill. I haven't fed on zebra, naturally, but I am aware of a slight sense of disorientation when I open my eyes. How long have I dozed? And more important, have I had my tea? Tea is like a Chinese meal, eaten and almost instantly forgotten. I search my memory and my waistcoat for crumbs from the fruit cake.

For me the danger hour is *circa* two-thirty, particularly if there happens to be a jackal in the vicinity . . . a playwright who has begun to read his script, a luncheon guest describing his avoidance of the South Circular Road, or searching the tip of his tongue to remember the name of the first wife of Mortimer Wheeler. It is no good explaining that I have been awake since nine. Umbrage is taken, tents folded and the caravan takes its leave.

To fall asleep when a friend is at the wheel of the motor is seldom taken amiss. The driver regards it as tribute to his management of the vehicle.

The luxury of an afternoon nap is a privilege of the senior citizen. Just imagine what the rest of the world is denying itself as they trudge around the snooker table or adjust the inflation figure.

There is, however, a real problem for those of us who, because of circumstances beyond our control, find ourselves up and about and far from home at the appointed hour and in need of a kip. Where to go? The club, alas, is not a solution for all, and one cannot be constantly donating blood and due for a short sleep with biscuits after doing so. In summer there is the park but it is not always a safe refuge. One is better off in a cinema or watching cricket. But here again money has to be spent. Not everyone can accustom himself to a church pew or to the hard benches of the spectators' galleries at the Houses of Parliament or the Old Bailey or indeed the humbler Magistrates' Courts. The armchairs have long since disappeared from Harrods. I cannot too highly extol Minneapolis, which in warm weather sports clusters of chairs outside the stores – but then one is seldom warm in Minneapolis, or indeed in the City. Gone are the news cinemas, the Turkish baths, even the opium dens. One is left with so little choice. There is no alternative. When finding oneself far from home after lunch one must try like everyone else to stay awake unless fortunate enough to be a member of the House of Lords.

> *"In bed we laugh, in bed we cry;*
> *And born in bed, in bed we die;*
> *The near approach a bed may show*
> *Of human bliss to human woe."*
>
> ISAAC DE BENSERADE

At bedtime I hurl myself out of my clothes, counting up to ten, but slowing the counting pace so that I win the race, even if foiled by a shirt button or a knotted shoe lace. The triumphant winner leaps into bed. Well, not exactly leaps perhaps, but the heavenly moment when my head is back on the pillow once more . . . ah! and one even permits oneself a small fart of triumph.

To read or not to read that is the question. Perhaps a paragraph or two and then a glance to the bedside table before turning out the light and the reassuring sight of the glass of water safely deposited there. Then happily I give myself over to sleep. Such pleasure, even though the realisation lurks that one may have to be up at least once in the night to visit the bathroom. Even awake at three, one contemplates with total bliss the prospect of another five hours of peaceful slumber. After all, one has to be awake occasionally to really enjoy sleep.

I have never actually measured the area which has given me so much pleasure but I would grade it as King Size. I have often observed how narrow are the beds of the famous. Old soldiers do die of course but usually on a truckle. When wandering stately homes and palaces I have been struck by how small are the beds of Kings. I seem to remember a time when we were bereft of the bed for a few weeks when it had to be resprung. Thank goodness it has now been back in service for years.

In my dreams I am forever missing the bus. There is one in which I am catching a mysterious plane bound for Le Touquet but it is always necessary to transfer to a small bus and go in search of an airstrip from which my journey is to begin. I am always pressed for time but I do seem to manage eventually to board, fasten my seat belt and wake up.

Alternatively I am on an operating-table and hiding from the surgeon a vital piece of his equipment – a highly polished telescope with which he wishes to explore my lower bowel.

Dreams come round more often to the old. Mine I am sure are about par. A last-minute decision to visit Mother in some remote village where she has lived for ages, during which time I have failed to call, results in my being totally lost in an apple orchard near Worcester; on waking panic gives way to a feeling of immense relief that Mother is dead and buried and has been for thirty years. Despite its occasional anxieties, bed is an abiding pleasure.

6
Getting There

. . . but can I read my notes?

6
GETTING
THERE . . .

"A little more tired at close of day,
A little less anxious to have our way;
A little less ready to scold and blame,
A little more care of a brother's name;
And so we are nearing our journey's end,
Where time and eternity meet and blend."
                                    ROLLIN JOHN WELLS

IN HIS youth and prime, Ninian Comper, the renowned church architect was described as a formidable figure, quick to criticise and take offence, but as a friend of his related: "He mellowed into a youthful and upright nonagenarian with a perfectly trimmed goatee and gold-rimmed spectacles, courtly manners and a voice whose exquisite modulation carried with it overtones of distant days of which he would talk with relish, when he dined with Beardsley, heard the news of Rossetti's death at Alfred Gurney's table or engaged in sympathetic discourse with Swinburne's sister, Isabel."

Ah, yes, the pleasure of sitting at table and enthralling a rapt audience with tales of the past. I find it a constant joy myself.

"You can only meet the Pope so often," I tell them. I have got their attention and the wine glasses remain poised in mid-air. "In those days, of course," I continue, "you had to go to Rome. He was a rather remote plenipotentiary of the

Almighty and I don't think had ever kissed a runway. The ceremony was impressive. One arrived early bearing the great white engraved card. It announced that Il Sua Santità was prepared to receive you in semi-private audience."

Now here one must pause, not only for effect but for thought. What actually happened was that for two hours we were shuffled like a pack of cards and then at last dealt with our backs to the wall of one of the various antechambers. The staff moved backwards with considerable agility and the Holy Father was amongst us, distributing small medals and considerable charm. I don't imagine he would have known me if we ever met again, but then as I said, we never did. It was a truly impressive encounter, but I wonder if the bare facts are interesting enough to keep the attention of my audience. A certain embellishment is, I feel, called for.

"It seems His Holiness insisted we take tea with him," I resume my tale. "He, of course, remained rather aloof on his golden throne balancing his saucer on his knee and munching chocolate cake. He was anxious to know about Anna Neagle of whom he was an aficionado. I was able to remind him that I was fortunate to have acted with the lady on at least two occasions. We compared her performances as Nell Gwyn and Queen Victoria. He was reassured when I told him that her marriage to Herbert Wilcox was all it seemed.

"I enquired whether it was possible for the Pontiff to visit a public cinema, but he told me he preferred to view most evenings in the Vatican premises; he had a cardinal who was skilled as a projectionist and they usually selected the programmes together."

The rapt attention on the faces of my audience around the table encourages me to carry on – too far, I fear. "When I suggested," I tell them, "to the Pope that I must soon be taking my leave, Pius demurred. He was so anxious for me to stay and meet his wife." Alas, my fancy has exceeded bounds. I have, as the modern phrase goes, lost my credibility.

Still, one of the pleasures of being old is name-dropping. I once reproached Simon Marks, co-founder of Marks and Spencer, for not stocking dolls' clothes.

"Morley," he replied, "I have re-dressed the country; they can make their own dolls' hats."

The conversations I have had with the good, the rich and the famous . . . But then most of us who have reached a certain age have our own personal recollections of the great, even if only viewed from a distance.

"Ah!" says a nonagenarian of my acquaintance as we meet at the newspaper stall and notice the name of the heir to the throne in the headlines. "I remember well the day he was born – and look now, little ones of his own. And doesn't William take after him?"

Once in Guernsey I was reviewed by George and Mary three times in a single day. We hurried across the island forming up as members of the Officers' Training Corps, as Red Cross Cadets and as Sons of Prominent Tomato Growers. The last was indeed farfetched in my case. As far as I know, Father never planted a single fruit. He had, however, evacuated his family during one of his perpetual cash-flow crises and there was a memorable spur of the moment departure at Waterloo after he had read that the Channel Islands were free of income tax. He enquired of the booking clerk which Island was closest to the capital. Only one return ticket was purchased and before a month had elapsed Father used it and left me to greet the monarchs. I was left with the impression that, although not yet on speaking terms with the sovereigns, so loyal a supporter as was hurrying to their presence in three such varied disguises would not go entirely unrecognised.

This was for me the beginning of a lifelong compilation of meeting with the rich and famous. Faithfully, I mentally stored away a list of those to whom on occasion I had nodded respectfully, with whom I had shaken hands or in some cases actually spoken. Mrs Roosevelt and I once figured together in a chat show. I met both Jack and Robert Kennedy, Helen Keller, Bernard Shaw, the already mentioned Pope, Anthony Eden, one Queen of Portugal, Windsor and Wallis, Garbo, the Queen, the Queen Mother, Lester Piggott and Graham Greene. I could go on for ever but must guard against my tendency to do so. The temptation to recall boring anecdotes of the circumstances in which I have encountered each, I do try to resist. Nowadays I have, I hope, learned my lesson, and when Field Marshal Montgomery's name comes up I maintain a discreet but knowledgeable silence. I smile a secret smile and nod wisely – intimating to all present that personal details about the great man will never be drawn from me. There is after all such a thing as loyalty. I shall at all costs maintain my silence, most particularly since I never met him.

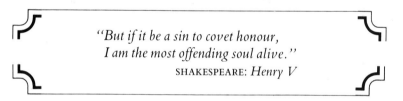

"But if it be a sin to covet honour,
I am the most offending soul alive."
SHAKESPEARE: *Henry V*

Once, on the staircase of Buckingham Palace I was questioned by an elderly courtier, clad, as I was, in a tailcoat. "Sheep or Goat?" he enquired. Afterwards we stood in long lines to receive eventually our gongs and then proceeded to the ritual display just outside the gates to have our pictures taken.

As one grows older one's chances of receiving honours improve. Meaningful careers in the Civil Service, the hospital precincts, on the concert platform or the golf course, the magisterial bench, collecting blood or shedding other people's do not always pass unnoticed.

Few may become Companions of Honour but a good many can pick up Honorary Doctorates. The night before achieving my first, we potential savants dined with the Chancellor of the

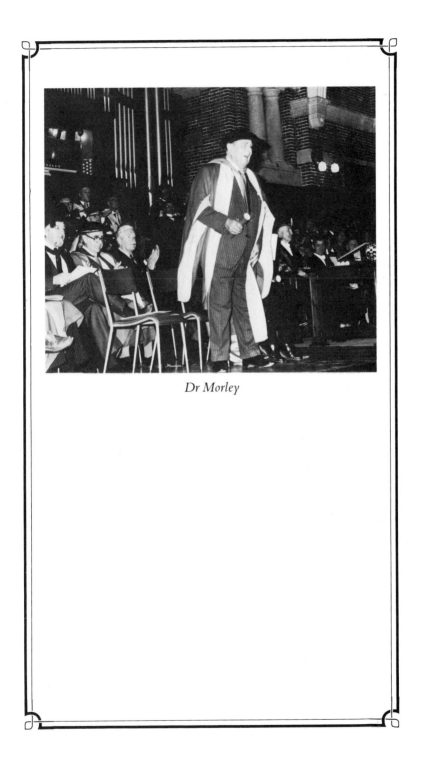

Dr Morley

University. Feigning modesty I asked his wife why I, a comparatively uneducated non-university scholar, should have been selected to publicly parade my wisdom.

"You live locally and haven't caused any trouble," was her answer.

Ah, the pleasure of the day. Suitably attired in academic garb I marched in procession paired with the Queen's racing manager. Seated on the stage, for ten minutes I listened to the list of my virtues, accomplishments, gems of wisdom and the titles of my earlier motion pictures. When the time came I raised my tam o'shanter impeccably as I had been instructed and was presented with a scroll certifying that I was indeed an Honorary Doctor of Letters. The robes alas had to go back to the costumiers.

Five years later I was invited to attend the installation of a fellow player. She was to be exalted to my high level. I was prepared, not of course to steal the show, but to be the first to congratulate her and point out that I was, for once, one jump ahead. I arrived at the university to find there were no robes of office awaiting me. There was no reserved seat among the faculty on the platform. I queued for a seat at the back of the hall and wasn't once introduced as Doctor Morley. Some pleasures are best not revisited. Too late I realised that if all Honorary Doctors were to return to their universities a population explosion must result each time a new lot is introduced.

"I shall go out with the chariots to counsel and command, for that is the privilege of the old; the young must fight in the ranks."

HOMER: *Iliad*

Having finished his *Glossary of Greek Fishes* the previous year, Sir D'Arcy Wentworth Thompson at the age of eighty-six flew to India as a delegate from the Royal Society to the Indian Science Congress at Delhi. His own work – alas, like its author, no longer in circulation – complete, he delighted in teaching and was still tutoring honours students from his deathbed.

Sir Bindon Blood had spent his working life specialising in signalling and in pontoon bridge construction. He spent thirty-five years in India and had military command of the Punjab. Seven years after his retirement, and at the age of seventy-two he was recalled to inspire youth. As commandant of the Royal Engineers he was needed to recruit volunteers for the First World War. But even then he wasn't finished. In 1936, aged ninety-four, he was the first officer to fill the re-created post of Chief Royal Engineer.

Then, of course, there was the wonder of Frank Benson with whom I had the opportunity to work when I was a young man. He appeared on stage into his late seventies. His genius lay in the opportunities he gave young artists to learn their stagecraft. His company became known as the nursery of the English stage. But I, alas, had delayed joining the company until it was a shade too late for us both. Sir Frank enjoyed to excess chats in his dressing-room with casual elderly fans. He was invariably late for his entrances but what was even more of a problem as he jogged along the corridors (Sir Frank never walked) was that taking advantage of the first available entrance he would completely mistake the role in which he was appearing. Each week he portrayed eight different characters and often when dressed as Sir Peter Teazle he would demand of Tubal the whereabouts of his daughter Jessica. Re-orientated not without considerable difficulty by the supporting cast he would leave the stage once more only to return in the near future to give his audience a taste of Caliban. He died like Henry Irving, in harness. Who is to tell an actor when he must quit the stage?

The museum director and bibliophile Sir Sydney Cockerell had been the director of the Fitzwilliam Museum at Cambridge for twenty-nine years when he retired at the age of seventy, but he didn't consider his work finished, merely changed. He settled in Kew.

"People will come to see the Gardens and look in on me afterwards if they have time," he said. And come they did. The young arrived in droves to consult and to listen. Although, when he was eighty-four he had a fall which affected his mobility, the 'Sage of Kew' held court from his bed for the next eleven years.

On location in Italy I once found it necessary, to counter the adulation showered on other members of the cast, to organise a small claque to accompany me up the narrow streets chanting "*Grande attore* Robert Morley". The result was that one styling himself a *'piccolo'* actor and not even on my payroll begged me for the secret of success on celluloid.

It would have taken more than my own command of his language to explain that understanding how to sell is the lesson any actor must learn. In my own case success avoided me for ten years, until tired of enforced unemployment I took a post selling vacuum cleaners from door to door. Even then I knew no immediate triumph but in time, and instructed by a colleague, I acquired the brazen effrontery required for both trades. My tutor was a genius at adaptability and a ladies' man par excellence: overcoming any obstacle to making a sale, including the husband of the customer. At times, when circumstances were favourable, he would satisfy the yearning of his prospective quarry not only for hygiene but also for romance. It was I who acted as lookout on the doorstep while sale and passion were consummated.

Of course my own dedication was not of his order but eventually he taught me confidence and I began to leave my clients, if not with crumpled sheets, at least with a hitherto undesired brand of New Hygenic System and a trade-in arranged for her own far more reliable vacuum cleaner.

Years later I met my tutor serving drinks in a bar in Acapulco. For some reason he feigned ignorance that we had ever canvassed together in the Tudor-style villas of Beaconsfield.

"You taught me everything I ever learned about acting," I told him. "At least let me buy you a drink." But he refused.

> *"Old men and comets have long been reverenced for the same reason; their long beards and pretences to foretell events."*
>
> JONATHAN SWIFT

For many years Alf Landon was the object of pilgrimage for aspiring American politicians. He lived past his hundredth birthday and was, right up to the end, happy to receive these acolytes and to dispense his wisdom. The fact that he had been crushingly defeated in his bid for the presidency of the United States in 1936 by Franklin Roosevelt seemed not to matter. What counted was that he had been there, he had seen it all and he had survived.

Whether it be the octogenarian gardener who regales one and all with weather forecasts based on prophecies culled from his years of observing the earthworms, or the elderly political pundit who has spent years watching the equally mysterious ways of the politicians and is ever ready to regurgitate his wisdom, the aged will have their say. It is a pleasure to share the past with those who have not been there and to foretell the future where one will not be oneself.

Halls are packed for the eldest resident's talk: 'Village life before the Great War'. Grandchildren have always been fascinated by tales that start, 'Once upon a time,' be they fact or fiction or perhaps a judicious mixture of both.

As for foretelling the future – well, I don't plan on being around to argue when I am proved wrong.

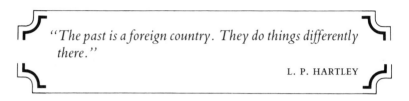

> "The past is a foreign country. They do things differently there."
>
> L. P. HARTLEY

Sir Arthur John Evans, being an archaeologist had, of course, an advantage: the past on which he was an expert pre-dated himself. At eighty he was personally excavating the Royal Tomb at Knossos, and four years later his major work on the subject appeared in four volumes. No matter what great age an archaeologist may reach he will always be a mere stripling in relation to his surroundings. His ninetieth birthday party was given by the Hellenic Society and the British School at Athens. Many gathered to honour his achievements and sit at his feet listening to his tales. He did not disappoint and lectured the assembly on the details of a Roman road he had just traced from Oxford to the South Coast.

Academics are experts at fêting the aged. Sir Gerald Lenox-Conyngham still held a readership at Cambridge University when the college celebrated his eightieth birthday.

"He is a scholar, a soldier and a great public servant and he looks all three," said the Master of Trinity. How very pleasing.

Gustavus Green was ninety-three when he had the pleasure of being made an Honorary Companion of the Royal Aeronautical Society. Winston Churchill was seventy-nine when he got the Nobel Prize for Literature. Violet Bonham-Carter reached the age of seventy-six and became the first woman to give the Romanes Lecture at Oxford; three years later she had the pleasure of being the major speaker at a Royal Academy dinner – the first time women had been allowed even to attend and she had the honour of addressing the assembly.

Who is to tell us then when to stop? Nothing is so frustrating as premature retirement.

"If they hadn't told me I had cancer," Harold Macmillan bewailed, "I would still be Prime Minister."

He was hosting a party of party-whips. I sat in the otherwise empty dining room of my father-in-law's club. After a time he too announced it was time for bed.

"Give the ex-prime minister the key and leave him to push it back through the letter-box – oh, and ask him to turn out the lights," he instructed the porter.

I suppose an ex-prime minister can be trusted with a simple task but in the end wiser counsel prevailed. My father-in-law pocketed the key. Sleeping, as he did, on the premises, he thought he would feel more secure.

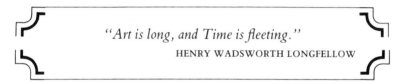

"Art is long, and Time is fleeting."
HENRY WADSWORTH LONGFELLOW

The art world has a two-fold interest in age. Many young and not-so-young painters are sustained by the task of painting portraits of those who have reached a certain nobility, a certain celebrity or indeed a certain age. It is a mark of honour to be asked to sit for a portrait and then for the result to be unveiled in the boardroom, the club or the regimental office.

The old should seize every opportunity to have their portrait painted – outside the National Portrait Gallery, on the pavement of Montmartre, on the Piazza San Marco among the pigeons; on privileged occasions, and at the cost of others, in the studio of an established portrait painter. He will be surprised and flattered, as I have been, by his ability to hold a pose. There is the fascination of learning that the artist will sometimes apply the paint not with a brush but with a rag saved from his discarded undervest; that a vast variety of hair is employed in the manufacture of paint brushes: sable, horse – even on occasion, pubic. But such details are even less fascinating than the sheer concentration with which one's personality and the colour of one's tie is observed and recorded by the painter. There is, of course, a problem. How can one impress the fellow with one's innate kindliness, humour and ineffable superiority? Each session brings a new challenge; conversation is discreetly pruned. Modesty is important certainly but at the same time the occasional achievement should be touched upon. There must be bonhomie at all times and once in a while the abject apology for altering the angle of the neck muscles or the direction of the gaze. There must be a good-natured acceptance of the artist's refusal to allow one to view the work in progress. Then there is the reaction on first presentation of the completed work! Praise! Astonishment! How those eyebrows have been exactly captured!

Then comes the half-hearted and cautiously voiced criticism of the neck. It is to no avail naturally. One is reminded of the final fitting at the tailor's. Whatever the hang of the left trouser leg no further work is contemplated. The chalk marker is no longer even in evidence. Congratulations purge the air. One is left with the canvas and the hope that it is not too large for the space above the fireplace.

There is much pleasure in being deemed suitable for immortality. Edward Henry Carson must have experienced enormous pleasure when he saw his effigy installed outside the Parliament buildings at Stormont. Even better than a portrait – a statue has such permanence.

Then, of course, the art world honours its own in a different way. Frank Brangwyn received a knighthood when he was seventy but that was as nothing compared with the pleasure he experienced when the Royal Academy paid him the then unprecedented honour of a retrospective exhibition within his

The portrait by Michael Noakes, 1964

own lifetime. He was eighty-five at the time and survived happily another four years.

Jack Butler Yeats was seventy-four when an exhibition of a hundred of his pictures was held in Dublin. The wonderful response to the show inspired him to even greater freedom and originality.

If Eileen Gray had not lived to a great age she would have missed the pleasure she derived from witnessing a really phenomenal resurgence of her reputation. As a young designer and architect she specialised in, and was applauded for, her lacquered furnishings and her abstract designs. When she was in her forties she was hailed as a decorator of rare vision and an architect of international modernism. However, time marched on and her reputation went into decline. The middle years were noticeable for the lack of honour they brought to her. Then at the age of ninety-two, her work was re-examined and an exhibition mounted at the Victoria and Albert Museum and at the Museum of Modern Art in New York. She found it very pleasurable indeed to be appreciated and happily accepted an appointment as Royal Designer for Industry – she was ninety-three.

The world of performing arts is also very good at honouring its aged. Actors are wheeled on to tell their stories about Irving or Kean. Aged actresses travel the world accepting a cheque here, an accolade there for relating tales of the early days in Hollywood. Everywhere there is at least a standing ovation. Survival is appreciated in the arts, both by performers and their audiences. Sometimes, it being in the nature of the show-off, things do get a bit out of hand. In 1778 when Voltaire was eighty-four, the production of his last great tragedy, *Irène*, was also the occasion of his triumphal return to Paris. He was not only greeted with the wildest enthusiasm but also crowned with a wreath of laurel.

Two centuries later, give or take a decade or two, Louis

Napoleon Parker reached the same age when he, too, experienced one of the greatest artistic pleasures of his life. His play *Disraeli*, which he had written for George Arliss, was filmed most successfully, and his story of Joan of Arc, called *Lily of France*, was chosen by the city of Nancy for annual production there. They, however, stopped short of the laurel wreath.

Nowadays those who reach a certain age in the entertainment industry are the subject of earnest interviews by film historians, respectfully *sotto voce*. They are the guests of honour at televised dinners in Hollywood where celebrities pop up and down from the banqueting table with pithy and often highly edited reminders of the recipient's talent, humour, genius and sensitivity.

There are those in the profession, however, not prepared to leave the honouring of themselves to others. Their pleasure is in documenting their own successes. William Poel, the actor, must have been adverse to honours. A most unlikely actor. He twice rejected a knighthood. He did, however, prepare a privately printed record of his own productions. He inserted photographs and notes which he compiled himself and presented it to his friends.

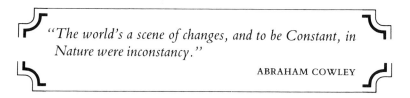

"*The world's a scene of changes, and to be Constant, in Nature were inconstancy.*"

ABRAHAM COWLEY

The enjoyment of longevity can often be stimulated by a bee in your bonnet. To spend one's life working for a goal and live to see it come to fruition is pleasure indeed. The chemist Frederick Stanley Kipping survived into his late eighties. It meant he saw his old, beloved college at Nottingham acquire university status. The writer, teacher and diplomat, Salvador de Madariaga, was elected to the Real Academia Española in

1936. Then came the Civil War and Franco's long rule. It was not until April 1976 that at the age of eighty he ended his forty-year exile and returned to give his inaugural address to the Academy.

The removal of theatre censorship in Great Britain in the 1970s encouraged that renowned farce writer Ben Travers to take up his pen again to write lines that would have been blue-pencilled in his younger days. He had a massive success with *The Bed Before Yesterday* in his eighty-ninth year.

I once embarked on a documentary to record the gathering of British Israelites. They seemed determined to survive to witness at first hand the Second Coming. Meanwhile, they slept, at any rate in the afternoons when the camera crew arrived. In the morning, bright as buttons, they foretold their own salvation and the truly horrific consequences to those who could not or would not claim membership of the lost tribe.

"You will be consumed in the flames," they assured me with considerable equanimity, "like everyone else. Only believers such as ourselves will proceed to the Pearly Gates especially opened for us."

"When will it be?" I asked.

"Today, tomorrow, but certainly in my lifetime."

"Is it too late for me then?"

"Much too late," they assured me.

Alas, in the afternoon the fire and the fervour were lost in slumber. In vain I strove to awaken them. Luncheon must have been a fuller meal than I anticipated. Briefly they opened their eyes and, perhaps astonished at the delay in the fulfilment of their prophecy, were lost once more in dreamland.

I went home empty-handed, at least as far as exposed footage was concerned.

Then there are those who are just waiting for the potholes in the pavement to be filled in or, like Malcolm Muggeridge at eighty-seven, doubtful that the bypass around Robertsbridge will be completed in time for his own funeral.

7
Generating Joyfully

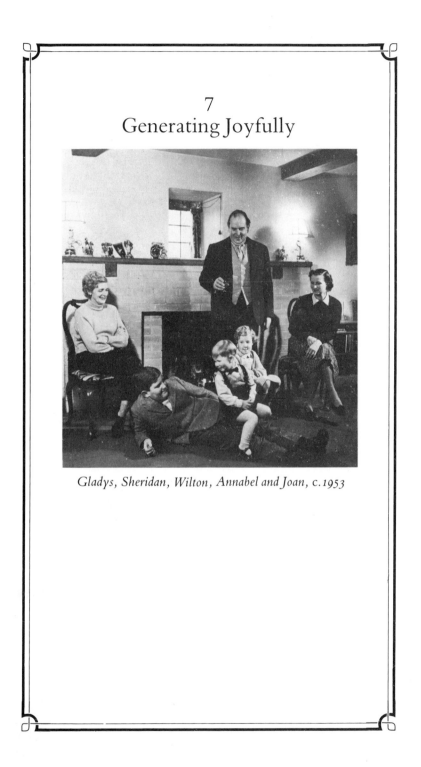

Gladys, Sheridan, Wilton, Annabel and Joan, c.1953

7
GENERATING
JOYFULLY . . .

> *"Every generation revolts against its fathers and makes friends with its grandfathers."*
>
> LEWIS MUMFORD

UNLESS YOU have bred exceptionally late in life, as did Arthur Hosier, the pioneer farmer, engineer and inventor who at the age of seventy-six married for the second time and begot a daughter, it is safe to assume that for most of us when we reach eighty or so our children will be grown up. A contented, if not necessarily a successful family is the supreme pleasure of age. Even if you were not the prime instigator of the blessing of parenthood your generation can hardly have completely failed to sow the seeds of posterity. There are nephews, nieces, even cousins or godchildren whose exploits may cause you to shake your head or nod it in approval. But, of course, it is your own children, if you have been lucky enough to have them and they have survived, from whom you will learn the lessons of life.

The time has mercifully passed when you occasionally reproached yourself for the mistakes you made in their up-bringing and schooling. Some puzzles still remain but your determination to solve them has slackened. It no longer seems strange that Edward, who seemed at one time determined to become a boxing promoter, should have enjoyed his life as a successful undertaker. Or indeed that Sybil who at the age of twelve was undoubtedly a prodigy at the keyboard and convinced you that every pound you spent on the Steinway and the piano teacher was well invested, suddenly lost interest and as far as you know never again played a single note. Had she fallen in love with the music master and found out he wasn't a bachelor as he claimed, but the father of four? Could that have been the reason? Too late to find out. Now she has that well-established dentistry practice in Wycombe. But on the other hand she never did marry.

To enquire about other people's children is seldom without a risk. Rarely does one discover complete success has been achieved. For everyone successfully practising accountancy in Woking or married to a doctor specialising in psychiatry in Lisbon, there is often one loose in the Himalayas or deep into Scientology.

The early confidence engendered by one's own child clutching the table and rising to his full height is often dissipated in later life by the discovery that by no means all are able to continue to stand or even to fall on their own two feet. One of the great blessings of age is that most of us do, and all of us should, stop worrying about them. One reason is that we have only the vaguest idea of what they are up to, unless, of course, they still live at home and are up to very little. But in the main they have pulled away and need neither concern nor advice. We do not love them any less. We keep their photographs on the mantelpiece, their toys in the attic. The rooms in which they grew up and to which they were occasionally banished are still called theirs.

None of us is good enough to deserve a child, as I once wrote in a play. That is still my belief although the director cut the line in rehearsals.

I have been lucky and although occasionally they have embarrassed me, far more often have I embarrassed them. I do have a distressing tendency to pull rank. Not all the time, by any means, but sometimes if there was a queue to be jumped I graciously identified myself and the children squirmed.

"It is not necessary to ring up. I will just introduce myself to the Floor Captain," I told my youngest when we planned dinner and a floor show in Las Vegas. Confidently we proceeded up the roped-off staircase labelled, 'Invited Guests Only'. The Captain, after a time, grudgingly acknowledged my presence.

"What would you be waiting for?" he asked.

"To be recognised," I replied.

"Not by me," he assured. "If you want a table why not join the line?"

You can't win them all, but my child had a ten dollar bill at the ready.

"Cheaper to have phoned, Pa," was his only comment.

Where grandchildren are concerned it is a mistake to voice one's misgivings out loud. The wise grandparents will soon learn not to expect too much. There is in the modern child an especially marked difference in mealtime behaviour. Grandchildren no longer accept the minimum of formality. One moment they are beside you contemplating the roast chicken on their plate and the next they have disappeared to turn on the television. Unless we are skilled at reproducing the conditions prevailing at a hamburger or pizza joint we find it hard to resist reminding their parents of how fond they were of steamed fish with egg sauce and stewed rhubarb and how they invariably asked permission to get down.

I have a grandson who comes to the house armed with a variety of fearsome masks and intricate toys, which only he knows how to convert from an ostrich into a Bren gun, and a granddaughter allergic to church bells, which cause her to emit high-pitched screams until the clanging, unheard by me, stops and the faithful are presumably gathered in.

Otherwise I get on moderately well with them. It is really no great problem having grandchildren. Most are returnable in the late afternoon and with luck the house is tidy again by eight. Never conceal from their parents that the visit obliged you to stay in bed the next morning until lunchtime.

Children long to impress their parents but seldom succeed. I took my father, a reluctant theatre-buff, to the dress-rehearsal of the first play I had written. It was a full dress-rehearsal; the scenery had been erected and the cast, which included no less personages than Marie Tempest, Sybil Thorndike, Rex Harrison and Margaret Rutherford, went through their paces. When the curtain fell I was flushed with excitement. Eagerly I awaited Father's comments.

"You think," he asked, "they are really going to do it then?"

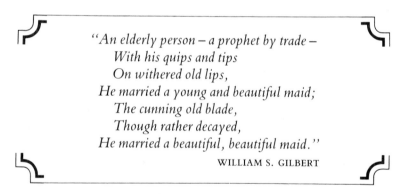

"An elderly person – a prophet by trade –
With his quips and tips
On withered old lips,
He married a young and beautiful maid;
The cunning old blade,
Though rather decayed,
He married a beautiful, beautiful maid."

WILLIAM S. GILBERT

A pleasure of age for some is a second or third marriage. There must be few who like the plant geographer and economic botanist Henry Ridley married for the first time at the age of eighty-six. And often the marriages are of contemporaries. Baron Beaverbrook was eighty-four when he married the widow of a friend and Charles Mendl, the press attaché at the Paris Embassy, married for the second time at the age of eighty. He had waited for his first wife to die. Although married for twenty-four years they were seldom under the same roof. Frank Swettenham could obviously wait no longer and after sixty years of marriage he divorced his first wife. He was eighty-nine when he remarried. Henry de Vere Stacpoole the novelist, who wrote *The Blue Lagoon* but devoted most of his life to the cause of sea-birds and the avoidance of sea-pollution, was seventy-five when he married his first wife's sister. *The Guinness Book of Records* lists those who married at age one hundred and three. And they are far from May–December relationships.

But it is true many men marry, if not their cooks, their secretaries, even their nurses in old age. Sometimes there are snatched ceremonies before luncheons; sometimes indeed the arrangement is kept secret – and the family subsequently await the reading of the will with apprehension. A widow who marries her butler or chauffeur; a widower who marries his masseuse or even his children's governess admittedly solves one problem but also confronts others. The period of adjustment by potential heirs, friends and not necessarily well-wishers can be prolonged.

Nancy Mitford summoned her father to a performance of her translation of the play, *The Little Hut*. He came with his housekeeper. Supper afterwards found Nancy well below her usual sparkle.

"What is the matter?" I asked. "You seem depressed." Was it I wondered that the elderly nobleman had accused her of not knowing the difference between a hunting crop and a riding whip?

"That was about my books. I don't mind fair criticism," she said. "What really depressed me was the housekeeper wearing the last of the family brooches."

Of course to find pleasure in a relationship it is not necessary that marriage ensues. It is not even necessary that the sexes should be mixed. Blessed indeed are those fortunate to retain at least one devoted retainer who has long since ceased to be a parlourmaid and is now a constant companion. My old friend

Peter Bull's mother was accompanied everywhere by her faithful minder called Jessie. One nerve-racking afternoon, for all concerned, they attended a matinée of *Waiting for Godot* in which Peter was appearing. The visit was not referred to for at least a week. Finally he summoned up his courage to solicit a parental comment and even then there was a lengthy silence. Then at last Lady Bull ventured a word of praise.

"Jessie," she opined, "thought the orchestra rail was quite beautifully polished."

> *"Marriage resembles a pair of shears, so joined that they cannot be separated; often moving in opposite directions, yet always punishing anyone who comes between them."* SYDNEY SMITH

James and Sarah Burgess lived to celebrate their eighty-second wedding anniversary and that is a record. Nowadays, of course, Golden Weddings are not uncommon. Soon it will be mine. I have been blessed indeed. Forty-eight years and my wife is still the supreme pleasure of my life. A happy marriage is a private joy. I do not think it wise to expose it in print.

Have I made her as happy as she has made me must remain her secret. She has lived with my jokes and my stories faithfully and unflinchingly.

When I returned from the theatre she waited up to ask what I would like for supper, but never the size of the house. Once when I returned from the accountant she listened patiently while I explained that I owed thousands of pounds to the Inland Revenue and we would have to sell everything even to pay half of the debt. She changed the conversation abruptly.

"The man came to tile the bathroom while you were out. You must ring him in the morning to complain of a botched job."

Our wedding day

"Have you listened?" I asked. "Have you understood?"

"There is nothing," she explained patiently, "you can do about the income tax. There is something you can do about the plumber. The number is on my desk."

On our wedding morning at a registry office we left our respective parents together in an outer office while we conferred with an official. It was the first time they had met.

"Is your father still living," the official asked her.

"I hope so," she told him, "I will go and look if you wish."

How often I have wished I hadn't spoken. How often I have wished I had just left it to her. Nowadays, of course, I do just that.

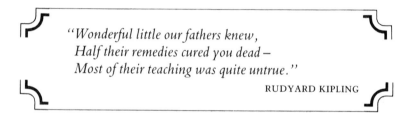

> *"Wonderful little our fathers knew,*
> *Half their remedies cured you dead –*
> *Most of their teaching was quite untrue."*
>
> RUDYARD KIPLING

One of the great pleasures of age is the realisation that there are no rules, no regulations that can guide you to a happy life. The secret of life is in living it. That, however, doesn't stop the aged from indulging in another pleasure afforded them – telling the young how to live theirs.

How life was enlivened for me in earlier years by Mrs Agnes Pope who positively forbade you to blow your nose in her presence; it was, she deemed, a very bad habit. A touch of eccentricity in age often demands attention and additional respect.

"Remember," your heirs will tell their children, "Grandfather cannot abide the mention of palm trees."

"Never forget to brush your teeth immediately after a meal with Great-Aunt Sybil. She keeps a toothbrush specially labelled in the downstairs lavatory."

As I was growing up I observed, in my extended family, at close hand, aunts and uncles who were determined to pass on the 'secret of life'.

Both my grandfathers were men of property of the kind pitied, and I imagine envied, by Barrie and Galsworthy. They left their families well provided for in financial terms. My father's father was Chairman of something called The Parcel Company and so he was the remote ancestor of the fearless motor-bicyclists who swerve determinedly and recklessly through the traffic today. All the children except Father remained solvent. Basil was a stockbroker who cried copiously at the mention of the Queen and on behalf of any of his clients who had listened to his advice about stocks and shares and had lost their money. He was cosseted most of his life by his happier sister who played the piano, but only when he was not on the premises. From him I inherited ten thousand pounds and a dislike of music.

My Aunt Connie was father's favourite but she married Edgar who wore stays and refused to lend Father money. Father sincerely believed that any member of his own or his wife's family who refused him a loan was genuinely of unsound mind and seldom hesitated to inform them of the fact – usually by telegram.

But Father's most formidable adversary was my Uncle Dolph who was in charge of the various trusts set up by my mother's father; he was Silesian by birth but had emigrated to South Africa and quickly – and rather mysteriously, it was thought – become a millionaire. Dolph's authority was absolute. He it was who imparted to the family the rules of life. He had a beautiful house near Newmarket which was filled with specimen tables and furniture. He was in love with the popular novelist, Mrs Belloc Lowndes. His was a religious belief in the sanctity of CAPITAL. To touch CAPITAL was for him the unforgivable sin. This belief he instilled in the rest of the family. He demanded adherence to his religion. As a result all twelve of them died with their savings more or less intact. (With of course the exception of my mother.)

But when Dolph himself died it was found that he had disposed of his house and the contents. He left exactly thirty pounds. No CAPITAL.

A pleasure of age – telling the young how to behave and doing exactly as you like yourself.

8
Gamely Viewing

Are you a winner, then?

8
GAMELY
VIEWING . . .

"The sports, to which with boyish glee
I sprang erewhile, attract no more;
Although I am but sixty-three
or four."

CHARLES STUART CALVERLEY

ALTHOUGH IT is true that there are exceptions such as Dimitrion Yordanis who completed a marathon in Greece at the age of ninety-eight and Duncan McLean who was still surviving the hundred metre sprint at the age of ninety-two, such aggressive activity is not a pleasure to the majority of the aged. Indeed it has never been a pleasure to me. I would never run a yard if I could help it; all my life I have felt the same, although I did once win a hundred yard sprint when I was forced into the race at my public school. Still, it was all downhill and I can't help thinking that I was given a head start. My preferred place was at the back. Coming in last you could see everyone in front of you. There is much pleasure to be gained by not sticking your neck out and thereby displacing your back.

It must be admitted that there are still those who will climb Mt Fuji in the ninetieth year or the Matterhorn to celebrate a seventieth birthday but these people are not the rule. There are less athletic sports in which the majority of the elderly delight. The Lord Chief Justice Alfred Lawrence took pleasure in landing large salmon in his ninety-third year and the Queen Mother herself is to be seen in waders. The first Viscount Ullswater was seen happily riding his white cob around Suffolk well into his nineties and Hilda Johnstone was over seventy when she was placed twelfth in the dressage competition at the 1972 Olympic Games. Eighty-six-year-old Betty McKeever most days enjoyed beagling, trekking across the fields accompanied by three younger gentlemen – in their seventies. Golfers of course go on for ever.

I prefer the gentle sports – a few underwater lengths, a mild saunter on the race course. Racing is a great pleasure, like the pleasure of collecting stamps. You think you are going to know better than the jockey, and you are certainly convinced you know better than the horse. Constantly one goes to the races and is proved wrong but the next week you are confident that this meeting will be the exception to the rule and you will go through the card. I often bet yankees. That means you must have four winners or two at least of the four and in all my years I've only won one yankee. That evening at dinner I lost track of the conversation as I was working out my winnings. The number sprang unbidden from my lips, silencing my fellow guests. It is quite a difficult procedure working out the winnings. You have to add one and then add your original wager all along the line. Mental arithmetic has never been one of my strong points, except when computing a successful wager.

Then of course there is the sport of watching. I began watching at an early age. Mother was a film buff in my formative years. Three picture palaces in Folkestone changed programmes twice weekly; Mother and I were there pretty often. Those were the days of the imperturbable Clive Brook and Warner Oland.

"This is China, Madam, where life and death are of no account."

Memory, no longer reliable alas, fails to recall the exact circumstance of the parting of the Red Sea.

Mother paid one-and-three and I got in for ninepence. It is a good deal more these days but I don't think that is the reason I am no longer an inveterate cinema goer. I was trained by Mother not to be late.

"If you can't get in at the beginning," she taught, "don't go at all."

Nowadays the pictures show at such mandatory times; and then again – is it the feature or the advertisements that come on at three twenty-eight precisely? I like to arrive with the lights on. The old are not keen on their footsteps being guided by a dim red light. I like to see the steps and who else is there. We never seem to be very many queuing to buy the cardboard drinks and ice creams. In Folkestone sustenance was brought to you at your seat.

Cinemas are places where I can still hear pretty well. The problem is in following the story. Senior citizens bewilder easily.

"We can't slow down just for them," film editors seem to insist.

I don't say I would like to return to titling – 'A week later in Monte Carlo' – I don't say it but of course I would. And woe betide us when the director edits. In those films I watched at Folkestone the cutting was done by the front office. When I made my first film in Hollywood it was still the rule. Then the front office was Louis B. Mayer. Menken once observed that no one ever went broke underestimating the taste of the public – or in Uncle Louis' case their ability to follow the plot. Nowadays most film producers go broke though I suppose that is not the only reason. Still 'Golden Oldies' aren't called that without reason.

At my time of life it is simpler on television. Reliable guides conduct me on tiger hunts or stand by as I witness the initiation rites of primitive bushmen. I follow with mounting excitement experienced gourmets sampling the delight of Basque cooking. Often they show me exactly how to prepare it myself. Indeed, as I have already mentioned, on the remote channels of cable television I even conduct a programme myself, which is all the more pleasurable since I cannot cook a sausage. After all the instruction I have received I am never tempted to try rushing to the stove and beating the eggs and lining the soufflé dish. Besides, there is another programme on now about how to make stained-glass windows.

I am not a great one for quiz shows, particularly when the winner earns a fortnight on the Costa Brava. Although no longer able myself to provide a correct description of an isthmus, the questions seem too childish, the quizmaster clothed with too brief an authority.

There is a shining exception – *Mastermind*. How do they think up the specialised subjects? 'The films of Laurel and Hardy', 'Portuguese history from the seventeenth century until 1910', 'the development of Bradshaw's timetable'.

I watch in silent homage but when the general knowledge begins I shout the answer – usually inaccurately. "Pass, you idiot," I chide, "they are all different kinds of *crabs*. Don't you know anything?"

Usually of course they are varieties of *cartridges*.

All you get at the end of a week's mugging and appearances at the Hythe Institute for the Deaf is an engraved flower vase and the congratulations of the Director General and to meet Magnus Magnusson. Still, I have pitted my wits against the best-informed ice-rink attendant in the world – thanks to television.

Pleasure for the old is in watching the others jump, hop and skip. It is watching others facing blizzards in pursuit of the Yeti or even old Uncle Bernard Levin enjoying his sauerkraut. He, like the rest, gives no hint that on his supposedly lone foray over the Alps he is accompanied by a sizable army of attendants cranking the cameras, lugging the equipment or perched precariously on narrow cliff summits, the better to record his progress.

"Then I thought of reading – the nice and subtle happiness of reading . . . this joy not dulled by Age, this polite unpunishable vice, this selfish, serene, life-long intoxication."

LOGAN PEARSALL SMITH

"A man ought to read just as inclination leads him; for what he reads as a task will do him little good."

SAMUEL JOHNSON

To be able to read what one wishes when one chooses is the great recaptured pleasure of life for the old and comparatively quiescent. Only the more fortunate, once they have learned to do so, were allowed to read what they wished to. Pleasure was interrupted at first by examination papers on the subjects others had ordained them to study. For those, like myself, who had difficulty in proving that the angles of an isosceles triangle were equal there was no let-up in the early discovery that such nonsense would be of no use whatever when we grew up; if indeed we were ever to do so.

In vain we protested we were not destined for architecture. No sooner had we learned to read in one language than we were commanded to read in another, a dead language preferably. The hours we spent poring over the Punic Wars!

Gradually it dawned on me, as it must on most of us, that for the remainder of my days I was expected to read not for pleasure but for pain. Thus are businessmen conditioned to spend hours at the desk slogging at company reports, internal office memos, balance sheets, prospectuses, other people's letters, filing cabinets, bank statements and the never ending chain of business communications in which they are inextricably bound. On their way to work they are permitted a brief respite afforded by the daily newspaper. Some might travel home clutching a magazine or a book they are too tired to open. For most of us the pleasure in the skill of reading became the daily grind until the blessed relief of age allowed us once more to recapture the excitement of *Comic Cuts*, the *Rainbow*, and even *Boy's Own Paper*.

Not for me now the neglected classic I once struggled with – the entire works of Dickens, the poetry of Walter de la Mare, Kipling, Shakespeare, Bunyan, Macaulay. I meant, of course I meant, one day to read them. One day has not come. Most likely I shall go to my grave entirely ignorant of *Paradise Lost*. My only excuse is that writing, as I have myself, I do not care to be reminded that others did it a great deal better, lest my own small talent and huge enjoyment should wither and die in the knowledge that everything by now has probably been said and written already.

What then remains? The newspaper, the magazines, and above all true murder trials and the detective story. There was a time, as with most men, when erotica had its place. This place is not so much in old age as in the middle years, and especially in youth; in those days it was the hunt that excited: in Paris the quest for the *Livres Anglais*; in New York where the Waldorf Astoria bookshop had the most comprehensive erotica library in the city. At home the hunt was almost totally confined to the back numbers of *London Life*, a weekly eventually closed down by the police at the instigation of Graham Greene, or so I have always imagined.

In the alleys of Soho pornography is still on sale these days. Visiting there the other day I found all passion to be chilled by the spectacle of racks of reading matter neatly stacked, sealed and labelled. 'Transvestism', 'Bondage', 'Spanking', 'Gay', even 'Jacking Off'.

The pleasure of erotica is covert. The brown paper parcel which the heirs discover in the bottom drawer to their embarrassment. When erotica came out of the closet it lost its romantic flavour. Wicked school teachers, strict governesses, even French noblemen, and confessions of helpless victims of their insatiable lust, of the nineteenth century, vanished in favour of explicit photographs and ludicrous letters from correspondents extolling the deviant propensities of their mates and enclosing amateur snapshots of their boudoirs and unattractive spouses chained to the bed-post.

Back then to the detective story. One is introduced almost daily in my case, to a new set of characters, a change of scenery, and a corpse. Often by the time the book is finished one has been introduced to several corpses. Who has slain whom? And why? Either you enjoy detective stories or you don't. You accept the formula or you don't. The current fashion is that the private eye is separated from his wife after whom he still vaguely lusts. However, he meets a bedworthy young woman and takes an acceptable rest from his investigative endeavours to bed her with a good deal of passion. He is continually in danger of arrest himself and he is not afraid to kill the villain in the final round after having walked into the potential death trap. The reader must only occasionally be one jump ahead.

Nowadays there are also women detectives, blind detectives, gay detectives and I myself once played in a film in which there was a dog detective. I don't think I would have bought the book from which the script was presumably fashioned.

There is a lot to be said for being read to – but not by myself, I hasten to add. I haven't the knack. When the children were in bed I was always the first to drop off. However, I was once employed in the cassette industry to read fairy stories by Oscar Wilde. Having omitted to read them to myself previously I was caught napping as usual. Too late I realised that Wilde was a great one for inserting his own stage directions into the text.

"How are you?" I would read and then dropping my voice dramatically continue, "whispered the fairy." Growls from the wolf elicited the same treatment. Somehow, the recorder coped.

"What do you usually say when we've left," I asked the producer as he thrust the cheque into my hand at the end of what must have proved for him a uniquely tiresome session.

"Isn't there one on which he got it right?" he replied.

I wasn't alone in defeat. I felt comforted.

There are now, however, available to us shelves of the works of others read by those more adept at it than I am. Talking libraries reassure us all that we are aging at the right moment.

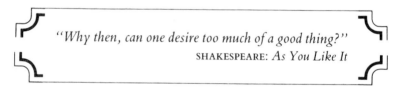

"Why then, can one desire too much of a good thing?"
SHAKESPEARE: *As You Like It*

There are so many ways for the elderly to indulge in the game of extravagance: First Class air fares, Perrier water, caviar, embroidered bedroom slippers, a permanent suite at the Ritz. A friend of mine once maintained one in London, another in Paris. For Monte Carlo she chose the Hotel de Paris. Once, on opening her bedroom door in the French capital she came unexpectedly on a porter wheeling out an enormous cabin trunk – the kind the Russians took to Ostend before the First World War. Marching behind it was no relative of the Tsar but one who looked to her like a salesman.

"Of course," she told me, "he could have been a murderer accompanying the corpse. I had my maid pack my own trunk that very evening."

Extravagance, in my dictionary, is the wasteful acquisition of objects and privileges unlikely to show a return on capital. I find it convenient on this as on other occasions to follow Doctor Johnson's lead in compiling my own guide to the language.

One of my happiest extravagances, much recommended to readers of this book is the acquisition from time to time of a young racehorse. This can be in my case a form of advertisement and occasionally partly deductible by the Lord Commissioners of Income Tax, but there is no chance of getting your money back unless you are Arabian or Robert Sangster and able to control the market. Even then it is highly improbable.

But to journey to Newmarket on a warm autumn evening, to forgo dinner and instead bite on a cheese sandwich and then to come home with a yearling you have arbitrarily selected against the advice of the experts, and often of your trainer, is an exhilaration of a special and a unique kind. You don't, of course, exactly come home with the creature. It is wafted away to be broken and schooled on the Downs of Berkshire or the sands of Morecambe. You go home with the cheque-book counterfoil and begin to test your genius in nomenclature. To find a suitable name – witty but with a hint of the breeding. And then you wait for your trainer's progress reports.

"He is jumping out of his skin . . . he is the best walker in the yard . . . he still needs a bit of time . . . he'll let us know when he's ready to run."

Then there is all the excitement of Wolverhampton in the late summer when he finishes ninth in a field of eleven – but he really started to race in the last furlong, you tell yourself. One day perhaps! No one ever considers suicide with a two-year-old in training.

Of course, to each his own extravagance. I was once doing a play about transvestism. A person waited at the stage door to thank me. He seldom, he told me, had enjoyed himself more at the theatre: it wasn't, he said, much fun dressing up when his wife was alive. She found it difficult to enter into the spirit of it. But now she was dead and there was no one left to criticise, to tell him that his skirt dipped.

"I've been really extravagant today," he told me. "There was the price of the ticket and then a bit of shopping. I bought some talcum powder and a rather elaborate petticoat."

Extravagance is a safety valve, a scourge to improve the circulation. To wake at six and count one's losses at the casino and realise that there is barely enough to pay the hotel bill but then to reassure oneself that the return ticket is already in one's possession. To unwrap your thirty-fifth silver donkey and hear your wife exclaim: "Not another! I can't believe it!" The bottle of bath oil . . . the box of chocolate ginger . . . the vampire bat model which dances when I pull the strings . . .

Extravagance, whether it entails the purchase of a new sponge when the life of the present one is by no means over, or adopting yet another penguin at one's local zoo, travelling first class by boat or air, or getting a second mortgage on the house and taking a stroll along the Great Wall of China and, if sufficient funds remain, constructing a folly of one's very own, is a good game.

Time was when I could have acquired a merry-go-round to site in the wood at the bottom of the garden but contented myself with a gypsy caravan. The grandchildren still sometimes play in it but the galloping horses exercise elsewhere.

How I would enjoy once more dressing up as Louis XVI and making the trip to Venice as a guest of Count Bestigui for the Carnival or joining Onassis on one of those yachting holidays to the Greek Islands. I am too big, alas, for small craft. But then a new sponge would not come amiss or perhaps a tiny jar of Gentleman's Relish.

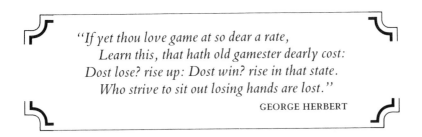

"If yet thou love game at so dear a rate,
Learn this, that hath old gamester dearly cost:
Dost lose? rise up: Dost win? rise in that state.
Who strive to sit out losing hands are lost."

GEORGE HERBERT

I don't think winning and losing have much to do with gambling. There are lovely old ladies at Monte Carlo who go every day. They take in a few francs to the roulette table and when they have lost whatever it is they take in, they stop.

I am convinced my father's ghost still haunts Monte Carlo. A happy ghost it is because his idea of Heaven was a spree at Monte. He never had enough money to stay for very long, but then sprees were never intended to last very long.

Although they keep moving the pieces and the Café de la Paix seems to have flown across the formal garden, the little town has not lost its charm, for me at any rate. Of course there are things to do while waiting for the casino to open. There are beaches and therapeutic baths and an aquarium and a royal Changing of the Guard, or one can simply sit and speculate on how long it will be before the skyscrapers march the last few hundred yards to the ocean and push the inhabitants into the water.

There are in Monte no bagwomen, no beggars. If the streets are not paved with gold that is simply because the citizens prefer to keep their money in banks. Everyone except myself has made a fortune, it seems, and stashed it away far from the reach of the taxman.

We had a friend of rather conspicuous wealth, one of whose husbands had once owned a railway in Canada. This lady used to invite us to dine in the casino but could never pass a roulette wheel until the number seventeen showed. She played in enormous *plaques* and often we didn't get to eat until the early hours, so intent was she in reassuring herself that luck hadn't abandoned her. Reassurance is what keeps Monte Carlo ticking over. It is one of the last places on earth where the ladies actually wear genuine jewellery . . . the spin of the wheel and ladies lunching in hats on the terrace of the Hotel de Paris.

A retired lady of my acquaintance on the other side of the Atlantic delights in subsidised travel from her home in Boston to New Jersey State and the seaside in Atlantic City. There she is also treated to subsidised hotel accommodation. This is all supplied by the friendly casinos. She enjoys the boardwalk, healthy walks in the fresh air and as a gesture of thanks deposits a few silver dollars in the slot machines before returning home.

Then of course there is bingo. Is it the game or the company that provides the pleasure for so many?

Card games are a great source of pleasure. The dealt hand was for me a perpetual excitement – to raise or not to raise? I relied on intuition, on knowledge of my opponent's character. To win the pot with a busted straight . . . to accept the challenge of bidding the grand slam . . . to go for tricks down, doubled and redoubled . . . those sharp exchanges with one's partner . . . how did I ever come to give up the games? The answer of course was marriage. My wife's attitude to the game was similar to the one she adopted later when playing Snap or Happy Families with the children. The main object was to finish the game, let junior sweep the board and get on with her other duties as a housewife. Losses on the swings meant in my case at least incalculable gains on the roundabouts. We still play Happy Families when the grandchildren arrive but there is a drawer full of packs of more conventional playing cards.

I have a few games of my own invention which bring me pleasure. These I will happily share. Never go for a drive without trying to make four-letter words from the number plates of other vehicles. Award yourself points for multiple words or three cars passing with the same letters in sequence.

This is a feat never achieved by me at least. If I were ever to succeed, would I stop the contest? Of course not. Does a golfer give up once he has holed in one or a pools winner desist filling in the coupon when he has won a million?

Another game I have played all my life and continue to play is taking omens. Watching the snooker, I say to myself: "If he pots that red I'll be dead in a year." Walking down the street I decide if I don't meet someone before I reach the next pillar-box something dreadful is going to happen – or something wonderful, I am, after all, in charge. I don't always fix a penalty – but if I do I usually forget it. Still there is that pleasurable frisson for a moment.

9
Catching On

Granddaughter Daisy, one of five

9
CATCHING
ON . . .

"Observe constantly that all things take place by change and accustom thyself to consider that the nature of the Universe loves nothing so much as to change the things which are, and to make new things like them."

MARCUS AURELIUS

"WHAT HAS changed then, Grandpa?" they will ask you, and you may find it hard to tell them. Not the weather certainly, but the climate in a more general sense. Single families, the bastard child is no more, the common-law wife is a meaningless phrase. Perhaps wars taught us not to take it all too seriously, to continue to break the mould. What concerns us now is not how others conduct their lives but when and if they will suddenly and without warning no longer be allowed to carry on with them, having been interrupted by kidnap, slaughtered by terrorists or starved by drought.

"Is the world a more violent place now, Grandpa?"

"No, more peaceful."

"A crueller place?"

"Kinder, far kinder."

"So everything has changed for the better then, Grandpa?"

"Wouldn't say so – exactly."

"What worries you?"

"Population explosion – and the other sort. But never mind that – join me in a toast."

"In Coca-Cola?"

"There wasn't any of that when I started. At least in those days they hadn't thought of bottling it."

"So, what is the toast to be, Grandpa?"

"To spies."

"Why spies particularly?"

"I always think they keep down the mischief."

"What else?"

"There are some things I could do without."

I could have done without computers. So could others in my opinion. Computers have added nothing to the quality of life. They have not decreased the workload but added to it. How simple it was once upon a time to claim your bedroom key in a hotel. The receptionist took it from its niche and handed it over. Registering as a guest was a simple process: not any more. You might as well be trying to book an airline ticket to Riga changing at Bucharest. The computer has to be consulted, the plastic card validated – and how often they go down on the job. The thing to remember about computers is that they can tell you nothing that you or someone else hasn't told them already. And how often they find the simple task of regurgitating information impossible.

Even if mankind continues the folly of computerisation, I know I shall be dead long before they invent a model which would be of any use to me. I would desire one on which I could tap out the simple question: "Where are my spectacles?"

The answer would appear in the magic mirror: "They have dropped off into the log basket."

I once tried to buy one, for the grandchildren naturally. It was a humiliating experience for the salesman and for myself. "Next time," he advised as he steered me out onto the pavement, "bring the grandchild."

I still have the last message imparted by the infernal

machine. "Ask it," I said to the salesman, "if I should take it home with me."

"No," read the answer. "You cannot teach an old dog new tricks. You would be happier with a ouija board."

I have stocked my own memory-bank over the years. Sections of my brain are scarred permanently. Instead of fresh thoughts which might delight, large areas are jammed for ever with meaningless jingles – 'The angles at the base of an isosceles triangle are equal' – 'Around the rugged rocks the ragged rascal ran' – 'Breathes there a man, etc, etc, etc' – 'Under the spreading chestnut tree' – 'Onward Christian soldiers' – and even my mother's favourite jingle is lodged permanently: "What is the use of a well without any water?"

What is the use of any of them, come to that? I long to be shot of them all. Perhaps I could transfer them to a computer and press 'erase'.

It is just possible that I could adapt more easily to burglar alarms. Some of my friends have them and it is by all accounts a growth industry. One has merely to remember the sequence in which buttons have to be pressed to halt the police cars in their tracks unless the cat has already speeded them on their way. The Monarch has recently installed lawn detectors at Sandringham and now the corgis are being trained never to bury a bone.

In our village there is already a watch committee. Once the prevention of crime is privatised the police will be redundant; meanwhile, however, it is difficult for the old, or even the young for that matter, to create a totally secure environment in which to rest a head on the pillow.

Most of us fantasise about the armed intruder advancing stealthily up the stairs; some indeed wake in the night to listen intently for the next step, for the door to open, for the blunt instrument to crash down on the sheet we have drawn over our head. I have a particular dread that the villain will be wearing a monkey mask. Of course if I have my head under the sheet I am unlikely to see it. After a time the terror recedes, as, still listening intently, I find the silence persists and I drift back to sleep. I find it a pleasure that I am as reassured by a sheet pulled over my head as I would be by any number of alarm systems. In fact, occasionally more so. I can control the sheet.

There are inventions, however, to which I still look forward. I want a substitute for buttons. An annoyance in old age is the inability to do up buttons as quickly as one could. Sometimes the struggle one has with a button is just perverse. How I long for someone to invent plastic magnets. Poppers can be as intractable as buttons, zips are not always appropriate. No, what one needs are plastic magnets. Inconceivable? So was a man on the moon not that long ago.

Greeting cards have proliferated since I was a lad – there are now cards for every occasion, indeed some for occasions one hadn't even noticed were occasions. Should I carry on sending cards? I am thinking not so much of the current crop but the old-fashioned Christmas variety. On the whole I disapprove of those who announce in *The Times* that they are not sending any but have forwarded a subscription to the Battersea Dogs' Home. I find inherent in the wish that all should enjoy the feasting a mild rebuke that the rest of us do not fully appreciate the plight of abandoned pets as they do.

I would be sorry if friends stopped sending them to me. I admire survival in others besides myself. I am flattered when I get cards from élite establishments such as the Ritz and the casinos I no longer frequent with any regularity. When one has lived to an appreciable age, not to be rewarded with cards is like requesting that no flowers should accompany the coffin.

The list requires the occasional cull, to drop some names belonging to those now enjoying Christmas in the sky. As usual, however, I find I have hopelessly over-ordered and am reduced to including some people I haven't as yet met but whose exploits have satisfied during the year. A card to the Inspector of Taxes and staff at the Inland Revenue may seem extravagant but at least it goes post free.

How shopping has changed since I was a lad. Although I am not allowed to shop in the local supermarket as often as I would wish, because I have a tendency to overload the trolley, I find the general mood is now so much more polite. Of course courtesy does sometimes cease at the check-out. Is everyone in so much more of a hurry or is it I who has slowed down? Which brings us to the vexed question of packaging. The enemy of old age is not death but cellophane. Nothing is any longer easy to unwrap. Has the health of the nation as a whole improved since everything became hygienically encased? With what happy pride one carries home the new toothbrush, but how does one get at it? Every packet is now a puzzle and, resenting the hours spent solving them, I now instruct the shopkeeper to open the new pair of nail scissors and pop them into the brown paper-bag – hence the queue forming behind me. I may prick my fingers but at least I shan't break my nails, or lose my temper. The elderly must adapt to modern customs but it must be admitted the eighties have spawned more than their share.

The truly threatened species is not the tiger nor the whale but the pedestrian. The motorist doesn't wish to knock us down. He knows that to do so will further delay his progress, but the driver of any vehicle must be counted as a desperate and frustrated creature almost as soon as his hands grasp the steering wheel and his fingers release the hand-brake. He may hate his fellow motorist but he positively loathes the unwary pedestrian who steps inadvertently into his path.

"Look at that idiot," he shouts, "doesn't he know this is a one-way street?"

One-way streets are often the root of the problem. The motorist's knowledge that he is travelling in the opposite direction to which he intended spurs on his aggravation. Thwarted, anxious to discover how he can navigate the maze and resume his journey towards his goal, he becomes increasingly reckless, his foot presses down on the accelerator and disaster looms. The abolition of the one-way street, and incidentally the circular route around Basingstoke, would serve to introduce the motorist to the rest of us travelling on Shanks's pony, and if not exactly grow to love us, should encourage a new world of mutual tolerance and respect.

I myself never pretended to be able to drive. My hand on the wheel was an open invitation to disaster. I attributed my lack of concentration and calculation of distances to never having been able to solve mathematical problems at school. A train travelling at eighty miles an hour will reach Bognor a good deal sooner than I ever expected. It will not, however, overtake the local branch line locomotive from Angmering and Chichester. Except for having to do the whole problem again in games-time I found it made no great matter. I wasn't going to Bognor and I certainly didn't want to play cricket.

When I took to the road the problem became more acute. I am no great judge of pace; to pass or not to pass posed a perpetual nightmare of indecision. Then again, I had a total inability to read a map. Motoring for me was an overlong and unwelcome trip on the dodgems. So giving up, surrendering my licence proved a most welcome relief. If anyone wants my company these days I have to be fetched and of course returned. The old can be a menace on the roads, stubborn in leading the charge, or more often the slow march. I know this is not a popular view. My mother-in-law, Gladys Cooper, used to boast she was driving when I was still struggling to master the bicycle. The secret of good driving, she told me, was courage and courtesy. She was forever waving to those who gave way to her on roundabouts.

"They have to," I told her, "just as you are supposed to do when approached from the right."

"I never heard such nonsense," was her reply.

The Englishman's home is his castle still but alas there is a temptation for the elderly to raise the drawbridge and not to venture out beyond the moat. This temptation must be resisted at all costs: get out and about and give the phantom mugger as good as he gets. Do I advocate having a go? Certainly. Carry a loaded umbrella and never be afraid to strike first. You may occasionally have to apologise, even make amends, but a courteous explanation will usually suffice.

At the New York World's Fair in 1938, Bell Telephones allowed free calls to anyone disposed to queue and ring Grandmother in Milwaukee. They also provided earphones for the public to listen in. Startled relatives once they had lifted the receiver always assumed that long-distance telephoning meant disaster was on the line. What happened? Why are you calling us? Is Frederick dead?

Nowadays telephone boffs call each other long distance to consult about a recipe for *sauce Béarnaise*. It is often easier to phone eight thousand miles than half a dozen, and so it should be – it costs considerably more. People phone from the swimming pool, while out jogging, from the car.

On a visit to the Stone Forest in China one of my children decided to discover the current state of the box-office in a Brisbane Theatre where he was presenting a play. He got through quite quickly, not to Brisbane but to Melbourne where the housewife who had innocently answered her own phone was naturally unable to supply him with the information he required. Then she learned to her considerable dismay that she was paying for the call. Her complaints fell on my son's ears to no avail.

"Calm yourself, Madam," he told her. "Your situation is unique. I would guess you are the only lady in Australia who has been in contact with the Stone Forest probably the whole afternoon.''

Myself, I have given up carrying the telephone when showing visitors the garden. Earlier guests called Papua New Guinea.

I have never been tempted to shut out the world with a personal transistor. I do not relish the idea of marching everywhere to the strains of *Lohengrin*, but it is true my own hearing-aid comes in useful at times. Not in traffic, of course, nor on a plane, but the occasional effort to keep more or less in touch is not always in vain. Manufacturers succumb to the increasing tendency to make them invisible. The tortoise-shell horn with the gold band is a thing of the past. Nowadays when they spot an appliance in the ear of the listener people have a tendency to raise their voices.

"Don't shout," I tell them sternly, "just speak slowly and enunciate properly."

Tolerance so frequently extended to the blind is not so easily afforded to the deaf.

"The old cow can't hear a word I say. Can you do something for her?" is the plaint of the average spouse contemplating the purchase of a deaf-aid for his lifetime partner.

We users learn when and when not to activate the appliance. They seldom work at cocktail parties and therefore spare us a barrel of unwanted information and interminable anecdotes. And we seldom hear the full tirade as the acquaintance driving the car has missed the turn-off to Newbury. He is satisfied with a grunt of commiseration and we are spared the details. Here earlier training stands me in good stead. Dispatched to Germany as a youth to learn the language I might just possibly have done just that but soon discovered the German word 'Zo'. When used sparingly this gave the impression I understood what was being said to me, which was seldom, alas, the case. *'Igen'* has the same function in Hungary.

The world, anyway, is divided between the compulsive talker, the raconteur (of which for many years I was one, alas) and the much rarer appreciative listener. The latter will never lack for friends and invitations to dinner. As deafness increases the patient remain in demand as long as their untroubled countenances do not signal a diminishing desire to hear what is being said to them.

As one grows older time passes more quickly some days than others. "Why do I feel so relaxed this morning," one occasionally asks oneself. Relaxed is perhaps not the right word; perhaps one was a little too active yesterday. A pause is indicated as one examines the activities of the day that has just passed. I certainly didn't get up any earlier than usual – a trifle later if anything. In the morning nothing untoward. Scribbled a few pages, enjoyed lunch and an unaccountably short snooze. I was wide awake by three I remember. A man called to service the water softener (what would Mother have made of soft water?) and another to point out that I could do with a load of gravel for the drive. Otherwise all was peaceful until it was time for the electric light and television and tea. In the evening a neighbour rang about her cat which had gone AWOL. After that I hardly moved from the armchair except to decorate the occasional tables with place mats. Bed at midnight and almost uninterrupted slumber except for the ritual visit to the bathroom to empty the bladder and replenish the glass of water. Now I remember it was the day before which had done the damage. I had had my hair cut, bought some detective novels, had my photograph taken in the drive, given away some prizes at a local school. I must take it more easily; ideally one should limit the action. One thing at a time. More and more one invites jet lag and the luck must turn, one tells oneself. I have completed forty-seven weeks in my daily paper lottery and still no prize – no five thousand pounds, no mini motor, no complete set of *Encyclopaedia Britannica*, no free passage to India. Oh, well, maybe next week, but I must try to control all the excitement.

I asked Stanley Holloway's son how gentle death had been with his father. "Very," he told me, "but he had one great regret, or so he said. It was that he never got the advertisement commercial for Mr Kipling's cakes. He had set his heart on it."

It is better, I thought, to carry through life one imagined sorrow than a multitude of genuine regrets. An uncle of mine by marriage fell head-over-heels in love with the wife of a colleague. Would they finally consummate their passion? Had they already done so? Would they eventually elope? We knew them for what they seemed: a deeply unhappy pair. Their melancholy persisted for twenty years. Finally death released them from their respective partners and they both lived happily ever after – never seeing each other again.

A friend had the perfect butler – except for one evening each month when he posted the agreed alimony to his ex-wife. On that one evening he took to his bed in a drunken stupor. When the wife died it took him only a few weeks to drink himself to death.

The old do well to trivialise past disappointments – others will take their place. The pleasure of the deep armchair may eventually have to be abandoned for a more upright one, but how much easier to help oneself from the tea trolley. The first duty of the elderly is to console not others but oneself.

> *"Contentment consisteth not in adding more fuel, but in taking away some fire: not in multiplying of wealth but in subtracting men's desires."*
>
> THOMAS FULLER

The most important thing to catch on to in age is self-satisfaction. The ability to rest comfortably on one's laurels, however sparse, is a practice much to be commended. A man who goes to his grave unsatisfied with his own achievements is not a happy mortal. If anyone happens to have a chisel handy he is at liberty to carve my epitaph – supposing he also has a tombstone:

> HERE LIES A SIMPLE MAN
> WHO STROVE TO DO
> THE WORK OF TEN.
> HAD THERE BEEN NINE OTHERS
> HE MIGHT HAVE SUCCEEDED,
> SO NEAR TO GREATNESS
> LET HIM LIE.

One can only do a certain amount. The old should not chide themselves. To chide others of course is a different ball-game and often a great pleasure. But no task one sets oneself is ever completed. We must leave the ending to others. Ours is not to mope; we have done nicely with the time and instruments at our disposal. Where we have left off others may or may not carry on, but it is important to be aware that one will leave off. Will the great novel now be written? Will the death duties be provided for? We must not fret unduly – better indeed not to fret at all.

10
Imagining

Home away from home

10
IMAGINING . . .

A LETTER TO MYSELF

Dear Robert,

Congratulations on your recent decision to cancel your instructions for cremation and the revocation of the desire that your ashes should be scattered on the race course. As you once so sagely remarked either you are dead or you aren't and it doesn't really help anyone to have your dusty remains scattered over the straight mile at Ascot even supposing the relatives can get permission from the authorities to alter the going ever so slightly.

Let me also pay a tribute to our heart, kidneys, liver, etc, which, although we occasionally assist them with the ritual of the morning pill, have stood us in remarkable shape and should one or the other decide to slow down or even pack up in the future it would be churlish to chide or cease to be grateful. After all, we have largely eschewed exercise, seldom abstained from chocolate, alcohol, sugar puddings, salt or pepper – nor have we indulged in any of the other reputed aids to longevity recommended by friends or the medical profession. Our confidence in our own organs being able and willing to cope with everything except perhaps cooked cheese late at night must have been a heartening stimulant to them. We have learned over the years that confidence in oneself is usually rewarded.

Such a pleasant contrast our life now is to that of those who rise at seven to deal with their correspondence, have scant time for the muesli, set off at eight to a television studio, spend a couple of hours hang-gliding and consuming a picnic luncheon in the clouds. They come back to earth for a conference at the Tower of London to arrange sponsorship for an exhibition of long-bows and then it is home to cook dinner for a small party of Japanese athletes here to popularise sumo wrestling in Cheltenham.

We, of course, are still in bed at half-past ten, lingering over *The Times*, having opened the post and decided not to answer correspondents from Milwaukee or East Germany in urgent need of a signed photograph. Soon we must get dressed and point our nose to the grindstone at the bottom of the garden and the first cigar of the day.

The bottom of the garden, perhaps two hundred yards away, is where the Colt House has stood for forty-five years and where we have written all we cared to write. You are aware of its usual state – the spent matches on the carpet, along with the ash and the letters and the copies of the *Spectator* and *Private Eye*. Tidy we are not.

But I don't suppose you have thought to mention that as we plod down the path, there is the occasional solitary lion that jogs up from the wood to meet us. Have you ever dwelt on the first of those gigantic birds alighting on the lawn which you have always feared would knock over the house? When the sky is filled with the enormous flock of pterodactyls returning to the earth they once abandoned there simply isn't going to be room for mankind any more. Not to worry unduly – *que será será* I suppose. And here we sit happily puffing and pecking at the keyboard until it is time to stop for lunch.

After luncheon we do enjoy rereading the papers, don't we? Especially on Fridays when we can check the local news and see if the ferret advertised last week has been successfully sold; then it is siesta and television and tea and television and supper and television and upstairs to tell our wife how the snooker finished.

But now it is another day and still no sign of the big birds, only the solitary woodpecker guarding the lawn. A lifetime of playing the fool – well, not always the fool. Wasn't I once Gustavus Vasa making an entrance from the back of the stalls in an Ascot hat borrowed from the director's wife and my first line, 'Do you think we've been recognised?' brought the great shout of unexpected laughter. Playing the fool – being recognised – anything more to show? This page perhaps, but at the moment it is completely blank. Is it the day when through the glass I spy the three policemen walking across the grass? They recur in my imagination. They are coming to arrest me but I am never quite certain for what crime. Enjoying old age perhaps?

Your long-time admirer,

Robert